RANKS & PRANKS

30 YEARS OF POLICING

COPYRIGHT

Names, characters, incidents and locations portrayed in it have been changed to protect those mentioned. No affiliation is implied or intended to any organisation or recognisable body mentioned within.Copyright

Author's Note:

This book spans more than three decades of Policing.

It describes the lifestyle, the sacrifices, the horror and the sheer fun I had during my career. These are only a few of the incidents I could recall out of many.

Events, locations and names have been changed to protect the identity of those described, and no affiliation is implied or intended to any organisation or recognisable body mentioned within.

The views expressed within this book are my own, and not that of any organisation.

INTRODUCTION

The time was about 0200 hours, the place was Redditch Police station. It was around 1986. Midweek things tended to be quiet. I was the controller; it was my job to dispatch patrols to jobs as they came in. The jobs were graded, either 1, 2 or 3, number 1 being an immediate response.

It was a dull night, and nothing much was happening. I looked across at the two Wendys, and we were ready to make the dispatch to a burglar alarm at Abbey Sports Stadium on the Redditch Road, a stadium with all the modern facilities of the day, including a running track. I picked up the radio mike and began the operation.

"Bravo Alpha 21, are you receiving? Over," I announced clearly, this being the call sign of the double crewed car which Jan was assigned to.

"Go ahead," came the reply. It was Jan, and she sounded eager, keen to get some action. Upping the tempo slightly, I instructed her to make an immediate response to Abbey Stadium, as the burglar alarm had been activated, and a possible break-in was in progress. "On our way," came the reply from Jan, her voice now sounding a little more excited, usually a sign that the adrenalin was kicking in. There was a tense silence in the control room as they made their way. In these circumstances it was normal for other patrols to pipe up on the airways, also wanting a chance to get their hands on the burglars.

Of course, there were no other patrols piping up, as they were already there, hiding, awaiting the arrival of Jan and her crewmate, ready to fall about in fits of laughter. Jan was so new, and green, she would not have realised that no one else had shouted up over the airways. I could imagine her becoming more nervous and excited at the knowledge that she was possibly going to catch her first criminal in the act. Minutes went by, and I was going to give it a few more minutes before I made a radio check to see if she was okay.

The two Wendys were giggling at the prospect of what was to come, when suddenly the radio crackled into life. It was Jan.

"Assistance, assistance! Foot chase, foot

chase," her voice was highly pitched, and her breathing heavy, a sign of the adrenalin rushing through her veins, but she was after all, chasing a suspect. A suspect who just happened to be one of her shift colleagues primed to run away from the main building on the arrival of the Police car. Every few seconds she bellowed down the radio that she was gaining ground on the would-be villain, her tone still as excitable and her breathing still heavy. If nothing else she was getting some good exercise. It was not until she finally brought him down that she discovered it was a shift colleague, who rolled about laughing, and was joined by other members of the shift from their hiding places, including her crew mate. Due to the excitement of the moment and her focusing on her quarry, she had not realised at the time that she was, in fact, running around the running track after the miscreant, and had actually completed a full four hundred metre lap before she caught her prey.

She took the prank well and laughed too, and made what was a rather dull night worth coming into work for.

This is one example of many similar initiations over the years, some of which I will reveal later in the book.

PREFACE

This is my story of my time with West Mercia Constabulary, nowadays known as West Mercia Police, from the time I first thought about becoming a Police officer. The fact was that I first applied to join West Midlands Police and was turned away due to my small stature. The story begins in 1975, June 23rd to be exact, and ends in December 2005, when I ended up walking out without notice, never to return. I had become a victim of what I am to this day still trying to figure out. I was either a victim of ageism, being on the wrong side of political correctness, or a victim of someone else's ambition to further their career, and I was seen as an easy target. This part is all explained towards the end of my story.

It's a story of one person's experience, mine and mine alone. In the book, I talk about the difficult times I went through, and the good times and the laughter, the camaraderie, the sometimes lack of confidence.

I was a mixed character, a marmite type of person. Some people liked me for who I was, others didn't. I was immature when I started. I lacked confidence, I was naïve, and I had no formal educational qualifications, most of my school years spent in the C stream classes, C being the lowest. I could at times become defensive and lack interpersonal skills. Some who know me would probably say I was a bit of an upstart. Some of those who know me well, of course, might still share the same sentiments.

There were others I met over the years who were in a similar situation to me, but I had a determination to stick it out and provide a comfortable life for my new wife and my son. I had a sense of what was right, and thought I could do good things by becoming a Police Officer. If it were today I, like many others I knew back in those days, would probably be unsuccessful in the modern Police Service. Today's applicants have to go through stringent interviews and assessments. The College of Policing now exists, and the Police Forces of today are looking for leaders, and qualifications, such as degrees and HNDs. Back in 1975 it was all very different, anyone wanting to join the Police would apply to a particular Force. There would be a standard entrance test, simple English grammar, spelling, and arithmetic followed by an interview with senior Officers. As I always tell people, in my day there would be a small advert in the Daily Mirror or The Sun newspapers, with words to the effect:

'DO YOU SEE YOURSELF AS A POLICE CONSTABLE? IF SO, COMPLETE YOUR DETAILS blah blah.'

I used to tell younger people that I filled in the form and I had a phone call asking if I could start the next week.

Another reason I used to give for joining up was that Policemen (and women) would be allocated free housing, no rent, or mortgage, which was also a good reason to join.

There was the saying by the older population, "Policemen today seem to be getting younger." Well I was one of them, I was not a teenager, I was coming up to my twenty first birthday, I was skinny, and young looking. Some said I looked about eighteen years old. This was true, I was still having to prove my age at some licensed hostelries when I was twenty years old. Of course, nowadays I see a Police Officer and can't help but wonder that they all seem so young.

This book will be revealing. As

mentioned, names and events will be altered or withheld where I think it is needed in order to protect both the living and otherwise. Some of the things I talk about will be surprising to the non-police persons reading this book. Those who are, or were, Police Officers, will identify with some of the stories I write about.

You have to remember the things that occurred in those days were accepted at that time, and are not necessarily accepted in today's Police Force, which is, of course, good for the service today. A lot of significant legislation has come into play, such as the Police and Criminal Evidence act of 1984, or PACE as it's known. This laid down the rules for the way prisoners and suspects are dealt with.

The Regulation of Investigatory Powers Act. or RIPA, which governs the way surveillance is dealt with, has brought changes, not to mention Health & Safety, which was non-existent in the Force when I joined, and of course, then came political correctness which has had a major impact. Some would say for the good, others of my generation would say it has gone too far.

The book will relate my memories of events that I experienced throughout my career. These events have not been documented by me, they are purely from memory and are events that stand out. The dates and times are sketchy so forgive me if I am vague about the timings. The events are a few only; there were many more, some of those events were insignificant and I don't propose to bore people with mundane subjects.

Nothing said in this book is meant to offend or portray anything that I believe is untrue.

So here it is.

Thirty years plus of coppering.

CHAPTER ONE
THE START- I WAS A LAW BREAKER

At fourteen, I was working for a local milkman at weekends. I used to be "his boy," as it was known in those days in the milk industry. The term was not a euphemism. If you used that term today, all sorts of innuendos would come out. All the milkmen in our area had boys working for them. I used to get five pounds for helping George the Milk, as he was then known, on a weekend. One of his customers was the local Police station at Shirley. The station used to fascinate me. Thinking back, it makes me laugh. George used to be so friendly towards them, drink their tea, then when he had collected his weekly money he used to make comments such as, "Bleeding coppers, never trust 'em."

One thing George the Milk allowed me to do was to drive the milk float. It was an electric milk float, with a top speed of about fifteen to twenty MPH unless you were going downhill. It was only on residential roads that I was allowed to drive it. He would be running from house to house with his crate of milk, and he would say the words "Bring the truck up," and I would jump into the driver's seat and drive it a few yards or so. I was about fifteen years old, and already I was breaking the law by driving underage.

I have a confession to make. I also broke the law when I was sixteen as well. In those days sixteen year-olds could buy and ride motor cycles up to 250cc. I and a few mates who I hung around with in those days went and bought our first motor cycles. I bought a Suzuki 50cc. I thought I was the bee's knees, and a rocker, a hells angel type.

In fact, I went and bought a second-hand leather jacket and put silver studs onto it to make me look the part, and there was a picture of the devil on the back of it. Looking back now I bet I looked a right dickhead.

I had a provisional license, and I put L plates onto the machine.

We were members of a youth club on the Cranmore Estate in Shirley, and twice a week that's where I would hang out. I made friends there and there was one particular girl, Sandra, she was a couple of years younger than me, (we still see each other to this day). She had her girlfriends she met there as well. One evening I said I would give a ride to one of the boys at the club. I can't remember his details, but he wanted a lift somewhere. I was easily led in those days, so I ripped off my L plates and he sat on the back. There was no requirement for crash helmets back then.

We rode from the club and onto the main Stratford road, where I was stopped by a Police car, and I tell you that my bottom started to twitch somewhat, funny noises coming from it, with a lingering whiff in the air.

I was a little scared, I can tell you, I knew I had done wrong.

Well, of course I had been caught and the Policeman reported me for carrying an unqualified passenger, and having no L plates. I didn't tell him my speedometer and horn were broken, and he never checked. My passenger? Well he told the Officer he thought I had a full license but he wasn't let off, he was done for aiding and abetting the offence.

I went straight home and I told my mother what had just happened, and she called me an idiot. Later that night the Policeman who had reported me came to the house. As I was only sixteen, he had a lawful duty to inform the parents. Two days later I was back at the youth club, mixing with Sandra and her mates. One of my main ambitions then was to, how do I put this, make a connection with a member of the female species, if you get my drift. Pop my cork, lose my cherry, so to speak, so any opportunity that came my way, I was happy to oblige. But in reality the opportunities were somewhat lacking.

One of Sandra's friends, named Vivienne, asked me to take her home. "Yay," I thought, "I'm in here." What she was expecting, of course, was for me to give her a lift on the back of my motorcycle. Of course, I told her I couldn't do that, having only a provisional license, and all that stuff, so she said I could walk her, which is what I started to do, pushing my motorcycle along. Vivienne lived in an area called Earlswood, which was in the countryside and about two to three miles from the club. I thought I would get back to her home and then see if there was any chance of an encounter of some sort, or at least a kiss.

We got away from the Stratford Road, and into the countryside. It was now dark, and as there was no one about, I told her to get on the back, since it was doubtful any Police would be about. Off we went, and her house was one of only a few on this quiet road. As I pulled up outside the house, there was a vehicle parked up, facing me with its headlights on. The lights were dazzling, and I couldn't make out what type of vehicle it was. It was about ten o'clock at night. Well, blow me down, it was a bloody Police car, and yes you guessed it, out gets the Policeman, but not the same one as the few days before.

"Hello young man, I see you have L plates. Have you got a full license?"

Well, you can guess the rest, he reported me for carrying a passenger and not only that, he went all over my bike and found the horn didn't work and neither did the speedometer. He booked me for that as well (Grr! George was right, bleeding coppers). Vivienne, she was let off as she didn't know I only had a provisional licence. Yeah right. I never even got a good night kiss.

I never told my mother about this event. She would have killed me and taken the bike off me. The next day I was at home. My mother was there and this latest copper turns up and comes into the house. Of course, I was now crapping myself. The conversation went like this:

"Has he told you what he's done?"

Mother replies, "What, do you mean, getting caught carrying a passenger?" "Yes," came the reply from the officer.

Mother "Oh yes, he's told me, he is honest, he doesn't keep things from me. Don't worry, Officer, you won't have any more trouble from him." With that, the Officer left, and my mother commented on how strange it was that two Policemen had been round about the same thing. I thought I'd got away with it until a few weeks later. A summons duly arrived in the post and I had to attend Solihull magistrates court and my mother had to come along as well. We got to the usher to report in.

"I see you are before the magistrates today for four offences; two carrying unqualified passengers, one no horn and one defective speedometer."

"Er excuse me," said my mother, "I think you'll find there is only one offence.

What's all this about no horn and other passengers? I think you need to check your facts." I had to own up to her, and she was not best pleased, I can tell you, I was fined eighteen pounds and had my licence stamped with three endorsements. My mother paid the fine and I had to pay her back £2.00 a week. So already I was sixteen years old, and had already been driving underage, and flouting the provisional licence laws. What chance did I ever have of becoming a Police Officer?

I first thought about becoming a Police Officer in my early teenage years. I used to see Police Officers walking the beat in Shirley, Solihull, the area where I lived. This area was covered by Warwickshire Constabulary, which was transferred to West Midlands Police in 1974 upon amalgamation of forces.

One Officer I remember was Sergeant Walker. I watched him one day in our local park, taking a lot of abuse from a man and his son. This would have been the late sixties or maybe 1970 or thereabouts. Mr. Walker stood steadfast, looked this man in the eye and never flinched. Mr Walker had a reputation as a hard man. The abuser backed down, and I think he knew he was onto a loser.

Mr. Walker was a well-respected man in the community.

Another was P.C. Player. Always pounding the beat, everyone knew and respected him. I am talking about the 1960s. The policeman on the beat was in my eye a man (most were men in those days) to look up to, a man who could protect you. If you were with him, nothing could harm you. I wanted to be like that. Strange, looking back in life, how events like watching Sergeant Walker can influence you indelibly and change the course of your life, because that is what happened to me.

It wasn't until 1974 that I plucked up the courage to go for it. I was twenty years old and working for British rail as a second man. That's the man who sits next to the engine driver, used to be called a fireman in the days of steam. I was engaged to be married to Anne. Anne and I had started seeing each other in 1973. She was training to be a nursery nurse and used to travel on the train from Solihull railway station. The wedding was set for August 23rd 1975. This date was set before I applied to join the Police.

All through my school life I had been in

the lower streams. (I wasn't what you would call educationally gifted.)   I never took any exams and on leaving at the age of fifteen without any qualifications, I drifted in and out of various jobs, from hotel work to factories, trainee chef and working for British rail, first as a porter at Solihull station (that's where I first met up with Anne) before getting a transfer onto the footplate at British Rail.

I was just less than five feet eight inches and weighed just above nine stone. I was a thin strip of wind, and I had suffered a bit of bullying in my early days at school because of my size. I never really let on to my family and friends that I wanted to be a Policeman, because they would have laughed at me. I lived on a council estate with my mother Minnie, stepfather Big John, younger half-brother little John and half-sister Diane. (I had two other elder sisters, Paula and Linda, and one elder brother Roy, not living at home). My Father and mother had divorced and both re married and my father had three children, my half-brothers Mark and Andrew, and half-sister Laura.

Although the Police were respected on the estate where I lived, they were, at the same time, treated with caution and suspicion.

In November 1974, I decided to apply to join the West Midlands Police, despite my having the traffic offences against me. It was shortly after that awful event of the Birmingham pub bombings. It was November, and I had earlier that day been at Saltley Engine depot where I was based, on the out skirts of the city.

I was courting Anne at the time, and I had been on a day shift, finishing late. At that time, the IRA were very active on the mainland. I remember I was either at home or just leaving work, and was meeting Anne at her home in Shirley, when the news report came in about the explosions in the City.

It was big news and I admit I was filled with some trepidation and fear. Most of the IRA activity was in London or Belfast, and I was worried that there were going to be bombs going off in the area where I lived. We had our eyes glued to the TV that night. It was reported that the Mulberry Bush and Tavern in the Town Inn had been targeted, and that people were dead. There were TV pictures of people running, and police and firemen running around, covered bodies lying on the street; it was awful. Only a few weeks before, I had been in the Tavern in the Town, a bar in a basement on New Street.

It was a worrying time, and a guard based at the same depot as me was killed as a result of the bomb in the Mulberry Bush. I didn't know him, but his name was Trevor. A few days after the bombings I went into the City, where I found other people viewing the bomb sites out of curiosity, and I was one of them. There were uniformed Constables standing at the cordon around the Mulberry bush, and I got talking to one of them. I don't recall his age, but I think he was perhaps in his twenties, older than me. I got onto the subject of becoming a policeman, what was involved and generally asking him about it.

He told me about the entrance exam, but it was one thing he mentioned that made up my mind to give it a go, and that was that if he could do it, then anyone could.

Up until then I didn't really have the confidence to apply. This was due to my insecurity, the feeling of not being good enough, having only a basic education and all the things that insecure people think about. He also looked important, standing there in his uniform, and I was thinking to myself, "I can do that, I want to be like him, I want to be one of them."

There was another time I had an encounter which I thought was terrorism. I had finished work at Saltley depot at two in the morning, and I was driving home through Birmingham, when the streets were quiet, my car being the only one on the road. This would have around the time of the infamous IRA pub bombings. It was a dry, clear night, the street lights were lit and visibility in the area was good. I'd just turned right from the Coventry Road onto Golden Hillock Road, a single- track road, that has one lane in each direction. There were a few terraced houses on both sides, as well as the odd commercial and retail premises. I was just approaching a couple of shops to my left when there was a small explosion in front of me, and the windows of the shop blew and shattered onto the road. Flames, large flames then appeared through the window, and the place was well alight, with smoke pouring out.

I went into panic mode and my first

thought was that a bomb had gone off, and I was convinced it was an IRA attack. There was a phone kiosk just up the road and I ran to it, my heart pounding as I dialed 999. The operator asked which service I required, and in my state of panic I shouted that a bomb had gone off and the place was on fire. I calmed down enough to give her the location, and I was told to wait in the area.

Within a few minutes the fire brigade and uniformed Police arrived. Local residents were now awoken by the event and were pouring onto the street. The Police placed me in a Police car, where I gave my explanation about the event. I hadn't seen any suspicious persons prior to the explosion. The Officers were talking on their car radios, and I was taken to Small Heath Police Station about half a mile from the scene. I wasn't under arrest, but was asked to go as a witness. At the station, I was left sitting in a room for about an hour, when two plain clothes Officers came to speak to me. The time was now about half past three in the morning. I was grilled about my movements, why I was in the area at that time of the morning, but as I was wearing my British Rail uniform, I was able to convince them that I was out and about legitimately.

As it turned out there was no bomb, it was a fire and the build-up of heat combustion had caused the windows of the shop to blow out.

West Midlands Police had only just been formed, following the amalgamations of several Police Forces around the country during April of that year. In fact, where I lived was now part of the West Midlands. Before April it had formed part of Warwickshire Constabulary. Parts of Warwickshire, Staffordshire, Worcestershire and Birmingham City Forces were combined to form the West Midlands Police.

My application was received and I was duly sent for, so to speak, to attend Lloyd House, the Headquarters of West Midlands Police, located in the centre of Birmingham. A grand name you might think. But in fact, it was an office block, which was and still is, the Headquarters of the West Midlands Police. I had to have a medical, then sit an entrance exam. I was extremely nervous and definitely lacked confidence. I didn't exactly get support from my mother or my future father-in-law, Ken, who incidentally didn't think I was good enough for his daughter and at times scoffed at me. In those days, he thought I was just an unintelligent yob, probably because I had long hair and came from the council estate. He didn't rate my chances and thought I was an idiot for trying.

I arrived at the headquarters and remember seeing all these other chaps, so much bigger than I was and who seemed more intelligent. This was my lack of confidence coming through. I sat there waiting to be called for my medical, which was the first thing. If you failed that you had no chance of sitting the entrance exam. I was called and in I went. It was the shortest medical I had ever had, and lasted two minutes. First of all I had to stand on a set of scales, which I duly did, and there was no second of all, that's where the medical ended. A Chief Inspector, who weighed me, said,

"Um nine stone. I'm sorry son, you'll have to put some weight on, I'm afraid. You need to be at least a stone heavier." I pleaded with him but to no avail. He carried on,

"You see, son, the problem is that if we accept lads your size, when it's a really windy day, the heavier Policemen have to go out and collect all the little Policemen like you in before you all get blown away." That was it. I never made the entrance exam. I was dejected at being rejected, but I was not yet finished. I was determined to get into the Police Force. Sorry, I mean Service. I thought up a cunning plan. Put weight on, that's what I will do. Easier said than done. (Nowadays I can't get the damn weight off.)

Well of course, the whole episode was a waste of time according to certain members of my family, and Anne's dad couldn't understand why I wanted to join.

"I get a Police house," I informed him.

"Well, you won't now," he said. He was right, of course I wouldn't. Perhaps I was dreaming, perhaps I was hoping for too much. He suggested I give up the dream, move in and live with him and Mary, Anne's mother. I was having none of that, because Ken was a very formidable and somewhat controlling man.

He was opinionated, bad tempered and he was always right and the rest of the world was wrong.

Over the next couple of months, I started

to take a liquid food supplement called WATE ON. I ate fatty foods, plenty of chips, and cream cakes. My weight increased by about five pounds. No matter what junk food I ate, I just couldn't put on that extra stone. (I wish I could say the same today). Anne and I continued to plan our wedding and our future. I continued working for British Rail. We started looking at places to live, and this became more urgent after Anne's Dad said,

"Why don't you both move in with me and Mary after the wedding? We can all live happily (unhappily) ever after under one roof." If that had happened, the marriage would have lasted no more than a week. We looked at the new town of Redditch in Worcestershire, only fifteen miles from our hometown of Shirley.

"Great," we thought, "loads of houses up for grabs," problem was that the occupier had to work in Redditch to qualify for one of these rented brand new houses.

Well, some good luck was waiting just around the corner. Anne had recently qualified as a nursery nurse during April 1975. We began scouring the job pages of the local papers and before long, Anne had an interview and was successful in her hunt for a job at a school in Redditch. She could start at the beginning of the new term in September 1975. Next, we applied for, and got confirmation from the New Town Corporation that we would qualify for a house, and the wheels were set in motion for us to choose one, and be ready to move in after our wedding.

"So simple," I thought. I was so full of confidence that I decided to have another go at joining the Police.

As Redditch fell within the Police area of West Mercia, I decided to apply to join them.

"After all," I thought, "I cannot be accused of wanting to join just to get a free house", which Policemen got in those days. "That'll come over well in the interview." So I sent off my application, much to the dismay of Anne's dad and my family.

"It'll all end in tears," they said. Within two weeks I had a reply. Because I lived within the West Midlands area they asked me to attend West Midlands Headquarters in Birmingham to sit the entrance exam. I thought,

"Here we go again." Six months had passed since West Midlands had rejected me. I went back to the building where I had been before, and my heart sank when I saw that same Chief Inspector standing at the weighing scales.

Of course, he didn't recognise me. I stood on the scales, just over nine stone. "I'm sorry son," he said. "Just a minute," I interjected, "I'm here to sit the exam for West Mercia, not West Midlands. The Chief Inspector pored over his papers, which confirmed what I had told him.

"OK son, but don't get your hopes up. I can't see West Mercia accepting you, but I'll let you sit the exam."

"Phew," I thought, "that was close, he sure knows how to instill confidence in a person."

All the prospective candidates, about forty in all, were ushered into another room. I sat at a desk and was handed some papers. This was it, the big test. I had to pass it, otherwise I knew what would happen. It would be phrases like, "I told you so," coming from my so-called supporters, in reality un-supporters. I looked at the first page.

"Spelling, great! I'm good at that," I thought. I remember the word 'beautiful' was spelt four different ways on the exam paper, and I had to nominate the correct one. There was a test on grammar and also mathematical questions such as 'if a ten-gallon tank takes so long to fill from a running tap and so long to empty with the plug out, how long would it take to fill if the plug leaked so much water a minute, while the tap was running? Well that totally confused me, and still does. Maths was not my forte. I still don't know to this day if I got the right answer.

I completed the test in the time given and the papers were handed in. We all sat there nervously awaiting the results. Eventually my favourite Chief Inspector came into the room and called out several people's names, but mine wasn't one of them. He asked those people to leave the room and they were escorted out.

"Crikes," I thought. "Now they've either passed or failed. More to the point, have I passed or have I failed?" My heart was in my mouth. The Chief Inspector fellow then spoke to the rest of us and informed us that we had all been successful in passing the exam. He then looked at me and said,

"You can leave, because I want to speak to all the other successful applicants about life in the West Midlands Police, and as you don't feature in that, you don't need to stay. West Mercia will be notified of the result, and no doubt you'll hear from them in due course."

I left that building thinking,

"I've actually achieved something in my life." I was on the way to the next thirty years. It was to be thirty years of adventure, camaraderie, satisfaction, excitement and boredom. Having said that I had to get through a medical and interview at West Mercia. Within the week, I received a letter from West Mercia, inviting me to attend an interview and medical. I had to go to the force's training school at Droitwich. Now this was around April 1975. I remember travelling from the M5 motorway at junction 4 along the A38 and seeing a West Mercia Police car. It was an Austin Mini Clubman, blue with white doors and the word Police on the two front doors, and it had a blue beacon on the roof. I'd never seen a West Mercia Police car before. Living in the West Midlands I was used to seeing Austin1100 saloon type Police cars. It did strike me as rather strange. I arrived at the training school, and it wasn't what I'd expected. A single-storey building, it reminded me of the H block prison in Northern Ireland, that sort of shape, I mean, not cells or anything like that. I believe the buildings were used during the Second World War.

So there I was, in my shirt and tie, and sporting a recent haircut, and, though I say it myself, I looked really smart. I was nervous, not knowing what questions I was going to be asked. There were other candidates there, and one stood out. He was older than me, about twenty seven, and he had long hair. I thought to myself,

"You've got no chance, mate, with hair like that." I was ready to tell them that the reason I wanted to join was to help the community, and reduce crime, and other worthy reasons. I wanted to make it clear that I wasn't after a free house, as my new bride-to-be and I already had the promise of a house in Redditch (which of course is in West Mercia area), and she had a job ready to start in September. The wedding was booked and everything was hunky dory as they say. Well I thought it was, but I was in for a shock.

I was one amongst several people there

that day. All, like me, wanting to enter the Police Service. Some were older than I was, some appeared younger. The medical was the first hurdle to get through. I was called into a nearby room and there a Sergeant greeted me. His name was Sergeant Ken Timmis, a slim chap about six feet tall, sporting a moustache. Ken Timmis was very nice and pleasant, and he was also known as the Drill Sergeant, responsible for discipline at the training school. He was a well-respected man and he went on to live a ripe old age well into his nineties. I believe he died in 2016 in a care home in Spain, when his death attracted many respectful comments on a West Mercia memories page on Facebook.

The dreaded weighing scales appeared and I had to stand on them.

"Er nine stone four pounds, that's not very heavy," the man said. My heart sank; "not again," I thought. "Still, never mind," the Sergeant went on, "I'm sure we can feed you up." "Great," I thought, and next came the height measure.

"Five feet seven inches," said the Sergeant. "The height requirement for the

Police is five feet, eight inches and five feet eight inches you are not. Right, son, straighten your back and stretch yourself upwards." I couldn't possibly have got any longer or straighter, and what do you know? Bingo! Suddenly I was five feet, eight inches.

Next came the medical with the doctor. The Force doctor was Dr. Laidlaw. I was ushered into his room, and there was this grey-haired elderly man, who turned out to be the Force Surgeon, as he was known. He ordered me to take off all my clothes and parade in front of him totally naked. I had never had to do this before, and I can tell you, I was embarrassed. He made me do all sort of things; stand on one leg, for example, touch my toes, at which point he stepped behind me and looked up my rectum. Then he asked me to cough, while he delicately held my scrotum. At the end of all this, he gave me a clean bill of health.

"Just the interview to get through now," I said to myself, "but not until after lunch."

After a hearty meal, I had to sit on a chair in the corridor outside a double door. It felt just like being back at school, waiting outside the headmaster's office. I was eventually called into the room, where I found myself in front of three men, two in uniform and one in plain clothes. The men in uniform were senior Officers, one being a Mr. Hodges, an Assistant Chief Constable. (He would be in this same room about six weeks later, but this time in a coffin on the day of his funeral. It was a strange feeling, actually, seeing the coffin at the funeral, and knowing the person inside it was the man who had given me this great opportunity in life to achieve something, to make something of myself; and knowing, too, that had he died a few weeks earlier, I might never have been given that opportunity.)

The other was a Superintendent. I never did find out who the third chap was. I was asked all sorts of questions, such as why do you want to be a Police Officer? what could I offer them? what did I think about Britain joining the Common Market? All went well until they asked about my personal life.

"I'm getting married in August," said I, "We've got a house ready to move into, and my wife-to-be has a new job." I continued to explain the circumstances, and that I didn't need the force to house me, as Redditch Development Corporation was seeing to that.

"I see," said Mr. Hodges. "If we decide to offer you a place within this Force, you will be posted to Telford. What have you got to say about that?" What a bomb shell! Telford? That was way up there in Shropshire. I'd never been that far north before, I was a young lad from the West Midlands. Shropshire to me was another country.

I kept very cool and came out with a brilliant reply.

"That's okay, sir, I'm prepared to do that, it means a great deal to me to be a member of Her Majesty's Constabulary," I lied.

"Oh God, what have I done?" I thought to myself. "Anne will kill me. Still, it will test her devotion to me."

"What will your fiancée say?" enquired Mr. Hodges. "She will stick by me, there won't be a problem," I confidently replied. At which point I was told, "You will be allocated a Police House. You will not be allowed to buy your own property," And with that, I had to leave the room and wait outside. It came home to me that the Police Force was indeed a disciplined career, a job where rank was important and to be respected.

Little did I know at that point how this choice of career would impact on my personal life, with its restrictions and expectations; things such as being told where I could and could not live, the fact that I had to have permission to buy a property, or that my wife would not be allowed to have any business interests if it affected or conflicted in any way with my being a Police Officer.

Five minutes later I was called back inside and offered a place in West Mercia. I was to start on June 23rd 1975. The wedding was already planned, and it was going to be during my training on 23rd August 1975. There was absolutely no chance of the wedding being cancelled, and luckily, we had not even thought about a honeymoon.

The day of Monday 23rd June 1975 soon came, and from this day until the same date in the year 2005 I would be one of Her Majesty's Constables, retiring at the age of fifty years and eleven months, and having the powers to arrest and detain. "Awesome," I thought to myself. I had wanted for many months to become a member of a Police Force. This is not a term favoured in this day of political correctness. Police Service is the preferred term nowadays. I would witness many changes over the next thirty years, some good, some bad and some I just didn't understand and still don't.

CHAPTER TWO
THE TRAINING AND PROBATION

The wedding was called off; well, for about ten minutes anyway. I had a right earful, I can tell you.

"What right have you to tell them that I would give up my house and job?" asked Anne.

"I told you he was no good," said her dad, "only thinks of himself,". I argued back, "I had absolutely no choice. I had to decide there and then, they were testing my commitment and determination. "They're going to allocate us a Police house in the Telford area."

"Telford, now where's that?" she demanded. We hadn't been far from home before, except for going on holiday to Wales, or Weymouth. Anne's Dad eventually came round and accepted the fact that I was going to become a Police Officer. He didn't, however, want any of his friends to know. He, like other working class men of his generation, was suspicious of the Police.

I supposed he thought I was going to grass him up now for all sorts of misdemeanors, not that he committed any. He was afraid that people would shun him. I tried to tell him that a Police Officer was supposed to be a pillar of the community, someone who people trusted and looked up to, someone who abided by the law. Well, it was like that in those days. But no, he was having none of it. According to him, all coppers were the same, they would nick their own mother.

"What an arrogant knob," I thought to myself, "given half a chance I would gladly nick you." But in reality it was him just being him a know-all. Now, my family was completely different. They were pleased for me and hoped I would do well. They never thought I would make it, mind you. I came from a split family. My parents got divorced when I was about six years old, and I was the youngest of four children. Both my parents remarried, my father had another three children Mark, Laura and Andrew, my half-siblings and my mother had two, John and Diane, with her second husband, John, who was a man I came to respect, and who was, in fact, now bringing me up.

The big day approached, and I had handed in my notice to British Rail. Thirteen weeks of intensive training was starting. I would spend my first week at West Mercia's training school, which was residential, and the next ten weeks at a Home Office district Police-training Centre at Ryton on Dunsmore in Warwickshire, before returning to West Mercia for a two-week course on local procedures. The training was classroom based, mainly on different aspects of the law, practical and role play exercises. It involved square-bashing, (drill training), swimming and cross country running.

I arrived at the Droitwich training school for ten o'clock on 23rd June 1975, sporting a smart (??) and short haircut. I wore a shirt, tie and jacket, and I had my suitcase with me, neatly packed with a week's supply of underwear and various toiletries. I was nervous and rather worried that I had made the right decision and that I wasn't entering an occupation out of my depth. I was not alone. Other men and women, all dressed smartly were, like me, looking on nervously. The men, also like me, all had short haircuts. We were all ushered into a room which was rather small, and I would have thought that the main hall might have been better. It was not to be, as Mr Hodges, my interviewer, had died suddenly and he was in the main hall lying in a coffin. His sudden death had occurred the previous week and his funeral was on this day. It was to be a grand affair by all accounts; a full Police funeral with uniformed pallbearers.

That nice Sergeant Timmins came into the room, but he wasn't smiling like he was the last time I saw him. He told us all to stand up, which we did, and the he gave us a pep talk about discipline.

"You're all Police Officers from today, and that means you will adhere to orders and discipline," he ranted. "You will call me Sergeant or Serge and anybody above my rank will be called Sir. Is that understood?"

"Yes Sergeant," we all replied. We were then given the house rules. We all had to be in bed by eleven o'clock, with lights out. Certain parts of the building were out of bounds; men were not allowed into the women's area, and women were not allowed in the men's area. Once we were supplied with our uniforms they would be worn, including the tunics, in the canteen at meal times, which would be classed as parades, so we were expected to be properly dressed and to be there on time.

"Well," I thought to myself, "it's like being back at school, or in the army. Still, I suppose I'd better get used to it." There were about twenty of us altogether on this particular intake, and we were all from civvy street, so to speak. I was one month away from my twenty first birthday and if my memory serves me right, I was one of the youngest.

There were about another fifteen recruits to join our intake, though these weren't civilians like me, but were Police Cadets. They were young men and ladies in their teens who, for the past year or two, had been full time cadets and were used to the regulations and discipline at the training centre. Now that they had reached the grand old age of nineteen and a half, they were eligible to become fully fledged Police Officers. They were going to join us civvies later in the week during the course. Once the pep talk was over I, along with the others, was given a room number, and this room was my bedroom for the week. We were all instructed to go to our rooms and report back later to get our uniforms. My room had two beds. My roommate was somewhat of a mystery; he was very quiet and he hardly spoke at all. I know him quite well these days as Lex. Lex would later in his service become a dog handler.

Later that day we were all given one complete uniform, which consisted of three blue shirts, clip on tie, a tunic, pair of trousers, a helmet and a truncheon. Oh, and a traditional Police whistle with a chain link. Everyone rushed back to his or her room, eager to try on the new attire. At last I began to look the part, except that my uniform was about a size too big. I pointed this out to the clothing store man and he acknowledged the fact, explaining that another consignment was due any day and I would be refitted. Until then I would have to manage. I looked a little bit like the comedy actor Norman Wisdom, who played a character called Norman Pitkin, in one of his films, In the film, Pitkin wanted to be a Policeman, but his uniform was far too big for him. The helmet just fitted, the side hanging a little over my ears; the tunic was too large, and when I had my arms to the side, my fingers poked out, but the rest of the hands were hidden; the trouser waist was a size too big and the arse end was baggy. Truth be told, there was almost room to fit another person inside the tunic.

I was a little self-conscious about it, but luckily none of the others took the piss.

There were one or two others with ill-fitting uniforms too, and at least I was able to get a properly fitted one a few weeks later.

After lunch, another pep talk, and the week's programme was explained to us. The funeral on that day meant our first day would be short. Breakfast would be at eight o'clock, and then we all had to be on the parade ground, which was at the rear of the building, for nine o'clock. "Parade ground?" I thought, "What's that all about then?"

The next morning arrived after a somewhat fidgety sleep, a lot of noise and shouting coming from the cadets' wing of the sleeping areas, and someone in authority shouting disciplinary type words at them. My roommate was still very quiet, not saying much at all. After breakfast, we all sauntered out onto the parade ground, where there were lots of policemen all standing in line in separate groups, Sergeants as well as Constables; all in their uniforms and wearing helmets. These were established Police Officers who were at the training school on various courses, and they were subject to the rules as well, and required to abide by the discipline rules of the training course.

A uniformed Constable who worked at the school arranged us new ones into some semblance of order, and told us that Sergeant Timmins would shortly come out and take the parade. Well, out he came, dead on nine o'clock, dressed in full uniform and wearing a peaked cap with the peak part slashed, so it almost covered his eyes. He marched out in military style; his boots were black and gleaming like glass. He came to a stop and stamped his right foot down so hard I could have sworn the ground shook. He then bawled out for us all to get on parade, and at that, everyone shot up straight and did what he did, with their right foot stamping down on the ground. Then out came some small bloke wearing a peaked cap, and wearing brown gloves and some silver things on his shoulders. He was, of course, an Inspector. The Sergeant saluted the inspector and told him everyone was present, and with that, the Inspector said a few words and the Sergeant dismissed the parade, except for us new ones. We were about to experience the art of drill. We were put through our paces and taught how to march. This is something I'd never experienced before. To me it was something I'd seen on the TV, with soldiers having to do all of this stuff. It was quite comical at first, we were a shambles, all wrong-footed and twisting and turning the wrong way, with Sergeant Timmins bawling at us all.

By the end of the first week, marching up and down was a synch, and a visit to the local Magistrates court had also been made, where we all had to be sworn in as new constables. We had to stand in front of a magistrate and read out some words on a card, swearing our allegiance to Her Majesty the Queen.

We had a tour of headquarters at Hindlip Hall a few miles along the A38, and numerous visits to the gym for PT. At the weekend, we were all allowed home. Then on Monday 30th June 1975 I was to report to the Home Office District Police Training Centre at Ryton on

Dunsmore. Our particular intake was large (approximately thirty nine altogether) and because of this we were split into two groups. About half went to Bruche Training Centre, somewhere up north. I arrived at Ryton at nine o'clock that morning in my Austin 1100 motor car and was directed to the students' car park situated somewhere amongst the many buildings. What I thought was the car park at the front of the main building turned out to be the parade ground, more properly called parade square, which is what I shall call it from now on. There were lots of men and women arriving for the start of this new course, which was to be known as 6 / 75. They, like me were all brand-new recruits from Police Forces all over the country. Some were ex- cadets, others were off the street like me.

Ryton training camp was a Home Office site. It comprised a main building, which housed the administration offices, assembly hall, bar and restaurant or canteen, whichever you like to call it. There were also two multi-storey buildings, which were fairly new. It transpired this was the female block, totally out of bounds to the men. That didn't bother me, though, I was due to be married in a few weeks and I wasn't interested. The rest of the site was like something out of a prisoner of war camp. The remainder of the buildings were old and, for all I know, may actually have served as a prisoner of war camp. The men's accommodation blocks, of which there were several, were all of similar design: single-storey brick-constructed buildings, a door at one end leading into a corridor, the bedrooms off on either side of it. At the bottom end were toilets and showers and washbasins, and that was it. Each bedroom had linoleum floor coverings, a sink, a wardrobe, a, chest of drawers, a desk and a chair; oh and of course, a bed. It was akin to a cell rather than a bedroom, drab and cold looking. The walls were plain and painted in a nondescript sort of eggshell. The windows were single glazed and metal framed, and although it was summer time then, I could just imagine the winter months would be cold.

This was to be my home for the next ten weeks, apart from weekends.

The first week was about putting us into our respected learning groups, or squads as they were better known. There were about twenty altogether in my squad, both male and female. There were four of us from West Mercia. Richard (Dick), six years older than me, Paul from the cadet intake, Jane, who later married and divorced Paul, and one other whose name escapes me. Others were from the West Midlands, Thames Valley, Leicestershire, Northamptonshire, Staffordshire and Surrey. One of the Staffordshire students was really old. He was at least forty, which confused us all, as he was well over the age limit. It turned out that he was a rejoin. He'd already done seventeen years as a Police Officer and then left for a few years and re-joined, so he had to go through the training programme again. His name was Adams. He kept himself to himself and didn't mix socially, which is understandable, seeing as the rest of us were mainly nineteen up to twenty seven.

We learned that during the ten-week course we would be required to go to different parts of the site for different lessons, for practical and role playing events, and we had to march as a squad to those lessons. This entailed getting in formation outside the classroom, being ordered to attention, and being told to quick march, and what have you. "How tiresome," I thought, but it was all part of the discipline. Each squad had to elect a drill pig. The drill pig was the person who shouted at us to quick march and halt, and to perform other similar moves. We chose Paul; he was one of my West Mercia colleagues who had been a cadet. He was a wiry slim-built person; he was an ideal choice for a drill pig, as he liked to boss us about, but he was used to marching, and that's why we chose him. He was to be our drill pig for the entire course. In addition to marching as a group, each individual was expected to salute an Officer of the rank of Inspector or above, when passing that person on the site.

The course tutors were mainly Sergeants, but there were Constables too, although it was hard to spot them, as they were allowed to wear Sergeant's stripes. Each Home Office centre has a discipline Officer, and that person is responsible for discipline and order. Ryton's was a tall, large man named Sergeant Trickett (he was actually only a Constable), and he was from the West Midlands Police. He wore a red sash over his tunic and across his torso, and a flat cap with its peak slashed. The shine on his boots, black and spotless, was like looking into a mirror, and the creases in his trousers were like a knife's edge. He was tall, well-built and looked every inch the part. He was a true disciplinarian, with a loud gruff voice that he used to good effect every morning for muster parade that consisted of a march up and down the square. Many of us over the coming weeks were to feel the sharp edge of his tongue. In fact, during our first week several students on course 6/75 were seen to leave the complex with their suitcases after a couple of days on the parade square with Mr. Trickett. He was not a man to mince his words and he certainly knew how to shout abuse at people; of course, it was all about sorting the men out from the boys and women from the girls.

My course tutors were Sergeant Glenn from West Midlands Police, and Female Sergeant Rhodes Hollingworth from Warwickshire Police. It was like being back at school. I was positioned near the front of the class, and immediately behind me was Dick, a twenty seven-year old West Mercia man who I became associated with for many years to come. I won't bore you with all the details, but during the next ten weeks I worked damned hard at learning and reciting definitions of criminal law, such as Theft, Robbery and Burglary.

I can still recite to this day some of these definitions. THEFT: where a person dishonestly appropriates property belonging to another, with the intention of permanently depriving that person of it; BURGLARY: A person commits burglary if he enters a building or part of a building as a trespasser with the intention to damage, inflict grievous bodily harm, rape or theft, OR having entered a building as a trespasser he inflicts grievous bodily harm or theft. At least, that's what I remember. I'm told it's changed now, especially surrounding the sexual offences, but that's not my concern any more.

For the first five weeks, our course 6/75 (every five weeks a new course started, so we were the 6th of 1975) was the junior course. Course 5/75 were the seniors. Because of the staggered start dates, there would be two courses at any one time. The senior course was always responsible for security during the evenings. This was designed to introduce them to foot patrols and use of radios. After tea, a particular squad would report to Sergeant Trickett and be given their duties. Basically, we had to foot patrol the grounds in full uniform and carry a radio. The duty squad also had to make sure that everyone was in their rooms and lights were out by eleven o'clock. No one was even allowed to visit the toilets at the end of their particular block. Thank God we had sinks in our rooms, which at least was a relief, literally! The duty squad had to be in their rooms by half past eleven. I don't really know who kept watch after that, I think the course tutors took it in turns. If anyone was caught out of their rooms after lights out, he or she had to report to Sergeant Trickett the next day. The punishment was marching up and down the parade square on your own in your own time.

It wasn't all work during our ten weeks. We had a few laughs and built up a good camaraderie. One of the students in our block would come and wake us up in the mornings. (There was a mixture of students from different squads) I remember he was a West Midlands Officer, but I don't remember his name. I woke up once and he was standing at the end of my bed, shouting for me to get up. He was completely naked, except for the Police helmet on his head and a pair of black leather boots on his feet. He would strut up and down the corridor dressed like this, shouting for us all to wake up. I could only assume that it was cold, that is all I shall say.

On another occasion, there was all hell let loose when the skeleton from the sick bay went missing. There was going to be an enquiry and all rooms would be searched. Well, guess what, it was found in our block. It was in Paul's bed, wearing a pair of his pyjamas, all tucked in as if asleep. Other mysterious events would happen in our block. Some of us, from time to time, would return to our rooms and find someone else's wardrobe or chest of drawers in there, or the sheets of our beds would be sewn up. You could be sitting on the toilet, when a half bucket of water would come over the top. It was a complete mystery at the time as to who was responsible. Then in the last week the truth came out. There was one prankster in our block, he was someone we never suspected, and what's more, he was someone we thought would be too mature to do such things. He was the oldest man on the course. Yes, PC Adams the rejoin, the one who kept himself to himself. He came clean and admitted what he had been doing all those weeks. Which just goes to show that men really are children.

At last, it came round to August the 22nd, a Friday. I was allowed to leave the centre at lunch time, because I was getting married the next day. My squad gave me an electric iron as a wedding present, and threatened they would all turn up at the church to hassle me. (They didn't come). I was to report back to the centre at nine in the morning on Tuesday 26th August, and no, I wasn't given an extra day off. The Monday was a bank holiday.

The wedding went well, Anne and I got married at St James' Church at Shirley in Solihull, with a reception at a nearby pub. Half an hour before the ceremony I had been in the pub with my brother for a swift half, a bit of Dutch courage, not that I needed it. The reception was at the Three Magpies Public House at Hall Green in Birmingham, a typical pub such as you'd find in any town. We weren't rich and couldn't afford a more exclusive venue such as a hotel. What mattered to us was that we were married. We spent our wedding night at 88 North Road, in Wellington in Shropshire. This was the police house allocated to me. My new wife was robbed of a proper honeymoon for the sake of my career. Now that's what I call devotion.

My proudest day of the year (apart from my wedding) soon came upon us. It was the passing out parade, and the last day of the course at Ryton. A day when all our loved ones would come and watch us march in unison to a live military-style brass band. My Mother was there, as well as my older brother Roy, and Anne's parents.

We were inspected by the Chief Constable of Leicestershire, and listened to speeches. Cameras were clicking, people applauding. I'd never experienced anything like it before. The day gave me a sense of achievement, especially when I remember all the criticism I had received when I first took on this venture. I would have to return in eighteen months' time for a two-week continuation course. But for now, we were all to report back to our respective Forces to continue our probationary period of two years. I still had a long way to go to become accepted as a fully-fledged Constable.

CHAPTER THREE
FIRST POSTING – WELLINGTON

At last, my days at Ryton were over, at least for eighteen months when I would have to return for my two-week continuation course. I was now able to go to my own little world at North Road, Wellington, and be with my new bride. After the passing out parade, Anne & I loaded up our little Austin 1100 and we travelled to Wellington.

Oh, what a joy, only eleven weeks before I had been living with my mother, a single man starting out on a new venture. In this short time, I had left home, been holed up at a Home Office training centre, got married, acquired a new home, albeit Police owned, and spent ten gruelling weeks studying and learning law for my new career. Looking back on it now, I can quite honestly say that I am quite proud of what I achieved. The discipline regime served me well, and instilled in me a sense of responsibility. I was due to report back to the West Mercia Training school the next Monday for a two-week local procedure course. This course was designed to fine-tune the training at

Ryton. We were due to learn local procedures in relation to paper work and other admin. After this two-week period I then reported to the driving school at Shrewsbury Police Station.

West Mercia's driving school had two bases, one at its training School at Droitwich, the other at Shrewsbury, and my course was going to last four weeks. If I passed with flying colours, I would be allowed to drive marked Police cars, if not I would only be allowed to drive unmarked Police cars.

I couldn't see the logic in this. The marked Police cars were Mini Clubmans and vans. Traffic cars were in a different league, they were high-powered cars, such as BMWs, and you needed to be advanced drivers, for which you had to do a different course. The unmarked cars were of the Morris Marina type, which were bigger and more powerful. Apparently, if your driving skills were of a low standard, then being allowed to drive an unmarked car was OK, because the public wouldn't realise it was a Police car. Yet if it was a marked car you had to be that little bit better, because the public would be looking at you.

The Police cars of today, of course, are the modern type, air conditioned, cruise controlled, the bigger cars with automatic gear boxes. Air conditioning in the old Mini vans was sliding the window open, and yes, I mean sliding not winding. Heating? Don't make me laugh. To keep warm in one of those in the winter meant wearing a pair of your missus' tights or thermal leggings, thick vests, scarfs and that's just for sitting in the damned things.

Between the 7th September and 19th September 1975, I attended the training school at Droitwich on my local procedure course. It passed off without event. Well, for me it did anyway. Some Officers didn't adhere to the strict discipline regime. We all had to be in our beds, with lights out by ten o'clock, as I recall. I mean, we were all grown men being treated like kids. A few Officers chose to escape through the dormitory windows, across the field and through a hole in the hedge. Off to Worcester City or a nearby pub, and return the same way during the night. I'm certain the hierarchy knew of their exploits. Of course, these days you tell young recruits of what it used to be like and they don't believe you. On completion of the course, a report was sent to our Divisional Commanders. My report said, "Constable Cherry views the Police Force in a dramatic way," whatever that meant. Probably thought I was some sort of Dick Tracy.

For those younger readers, Dick Tracy was a fictional comic character, a tough and intelligent detective.

On the 22nd September 1975, I reported to the driving school at Shrewsbury Police station. I had to spend the next two or four weeks (I can't quite remember how long) learning to drive in a professional manner, and to a higher standard than the average motorist. Well, that was the plan anyway, and it was an enjoyable two or four weeks. Our instructor was a civilian named Des Bowen. The first week of the course caused some slight discomfort to my upper left arm. Mind you, it wasn't just me who suffered this symptom; the other two Officers with me also experienced pain and discomfort in the same region. I think it might have been something to do with the fact that if you lowered your left hand from the ten to two position on the steering wheel, or held on to the gear knob while driving, you got a thump in the arm from Des. This same technique came in useful in later years, when I gave lessons to my son.

By this time, I'd been a Police Officer for three months, and I had yet to taste the reality of this, as I had not yet been out on the streets or had any contact with the public. Even when the course was over I still had to spend some time with an experienced Constable (Parent Constable as it was known) before being let loose on my own. I did, however, get a small taster of real Police work during the driving course. The vehicle we were using was in fact an unmarked vehicle, and as such, it didn't possess any blue lights or two-tone horns, but it did have a radio linked to Headquarters.

We were in the Shrewsbury area and it was at a time when the IRA were very active in the UK (due to the Northern Ireland troubles.) A call came over the radio for local Officers to attend a large department store in the town centre, which had received a bomb warning. Now strictly speaking, our car would not normally get involved as we were, after all, inexperienced recruits.

Des asked if we wanted to go and assist in the search. Well, it was like asking a small child if he wanted a bag of sweets. "You bet," we said, so the instructor insisted that he drove, and by God, what a drive. With headlights on full beam in broad daylight, and hand on and off the horn, we raced through the streets of Shrewsbury to the amazement of pedestrians and other motorists alike. There was also the sound of two tones in the distance from other attending Police cars. I was in a quiet state of excitement, the adrenaline was pumping, and I thought, "Yes this is what it's all about, at last I am a proper policeman." (Maybe the assessment from the training school was right, I was dramatic). We arrived at the store, and with other attending Officers, we began to make a search of the shop area, from which the public had already been cleared. It was a proud moment; there I was in full uniform doing a proper Policeman-like job.

As it turned out, nothing was found and within half an hour we were back to the arm-thumping routine. A bit of an anti-climax really when I look back.

With the course over, I learned that I'd

passed my Panda test, i.e. I was allowed to drive marked cars up to a certain engine size, which was 1800cc. I was reported on; in those days, you were reported on everything you did. My report said, "Constable Cherry drove quite well, but the danger of excessive speed needed to be pointed out to him." So, with my driving wings under my belt, I was now looking forward to going to my posted Station at Wellington in Shropshire to start some real Policing.

I had met my tutor Constable, who was to hold my hand for the next few weeks. He actually came to my Police house one evening to introduce himself and have a cup of tea. His name was Rick. I'll never forget the night I answered the door and saw this uniformed Officer, helmet on his head, standing there. For a moment, I forgot I was a Policeman and when I saw him I thought, "Blimey what have I done, why is a policeman knocking on my door, what will the neighbour think?"

When the weekend was over, I was both excited and apprehensive about my first day on Division which was the 6th October 1975. I teamed up with Rick, who was a beat Officer and not a shift Officer. Beat officers were known as RBOs (Residential Beat Officer). It's a good idea to explain the difference for those not familiar with the jargon. A beat Officer is one who patrols the same 'patch', be it an estate or a small geographic area. He or she would be expected to get to know the community and its criminal fraternity. They would generally work between eight o'clock in the morning and midnight. A shift Officer (there would be four shifts in all, covering the 24-hour day, or squads as they were known at Wellington) would patrol areas on foot or in cars and respond to the public's request for assistance. They would not necessarily be patrolling the same area every day. Every few years the same format would more or less apply, but the management, or someone trying to make a name for themselves, would rename the role from RBO to Beat Manager or Safer Neighborhood Teams, or Sector Policing: just reinventing the wheel.

My first day was spent around the station, getting to know where the different departments were, such as CID or admin. The Collator was the was the man or woman who kept files and intelligence information on known criminals and their activities. All this information was on a card index, West Mercia didn't have computers or tablets, there was no digital age. No CCTV, it was all hand written, there was a typing pool of ladies typing statement and reports, there were probably one or two type writers in the report writing room that worked, or that still had some ink on the ribbon. The Police National Computer (housed in London and used by all Forces) had only just come into use.

The PNC was an up-to-date modern data base that in those days only recorded stolen vehicles. Only the Force Operations room at Hindlip had access to the PNC. We could check registration numbers over the Force radio, or if we were in an office, we could do it via a telephone call. Around the UK there were regional Criminal Record Offices dotted about, the one for our area was called MIDCRO, based in Birmingham. Before the PNC was in full use, any convicttion records, fingerprints, or details of stolen vehicles were held at MIDCRO (as well as force HQ for local stuff).

A year or so before I joined, if we wanted to check if a vehicle was stolen, the radio operator would make a phone call to MIDCRO, who would look through a card index, before we got a result back. So we were waiting around for several minutes for the result. With the PNC, it was almost an instant response. The PNC went on to store a large data base on all criminal records and convictions. The list is now quite long, and on top of that, today's Officers can check if vehicles have insurance and MOT. The first computer system I remember being installed in station control rooms, was a system called CIFS, and this stood for Criminal Intelligence and Firearm System. It was a West Mercia System. The intelligence part was the start of the demise of the role of the Collator, the Firearms part was the data showing all those persons in West Mercia who held a shotgun or firearm certificate. After the role of the Collator, came Divisional Intelligence departments who employed civilian clerks as well as warranted Officers, whose role was to identify active criminals through intelligence, and prepare packages to target them.

I also had the pleasure of meeting the Deputy Head of the Division, Superintendent Glover. Mr Glover was a tall, large man, with a small moustache, who stood very upright and I could imagine him as an ex-guardsmen and a strict disciplinarian. I stood outside his office with my helmet on my head. The moment I entered his office, I had to march up to his desk, salute and stand to attention until he told me to stand easy (relax). If you told a young officer of today what it was like then, they wouldn't believe you. He gave me his spiel about having to work hard, be loyal and to be disciplined. He finished off by telling me that if I ever came before him for misbehaviour or for letting the Constabulary down he would, "String me up by …."!! well you can imagine, bless him.

The team I joined was known as Squad Three, a mixture of new and old Constables. There was an Inspector in charge named Ron Whittle and two Sergeants, Ron Gilbert and Frank Carsley. Gilbert and Carsley were old-timers coming to the end of their service. Crikey, thinking about it now, they must have joined before I was born in 1954. Frank was a large man with a head of white hair. I would have put him at about fifty. In my eyes, he looked too old to still be in the Force. Frank's role was that of Station Sergeant. He was responsible for the public counter and the radio room, which was normally staffed by one support person (civilian) and maybe one Constable. A far cry from these days of call centres and hi-tech systems. He was also responsible for the welfare and supervision of the cell area and prisoners. Wellington had six cells in all.

This was before the introduction of the Custody Sergeant, (among many other rules to make it "fair" to the suspects) brought about by the Police and Criminal Evidence act 1984. (PACE). Ron was of a similar age, six-foot-tall with dark hair and wore glasses, which always seemed to be perched on the edge of his nose. He would look at you by peering over the top. Ron had many years of CID experience, and he was once attached to the Regional Crime Squad in the Midlands area. He was not a well man and he suffered from heart problems. Despite his health, he was the Patrol Sergeant. His role consisted of supervising the Constables out there on the streets. He would tell us our duties for the day, allocate our refreshment times and check all our paper work. In addition, he would ensure that probationers like me would be working hard and learning the practical side of the role of Constable. Both Sergeants were responsible to the shift Inspector, Mr. Whittle. Inspector Whittle was an unassuming sort of man. He was younger than the two Sergeants, though not by much. I didn't have much contact with him really, and he was only my Inspector for a short while. A newly promoted Inspector was soon to arrive at Wellington, a much younger man than Frank and Ron. His name was David. He was a real, hard-working and excellent thief catcher, very sure of himself, and he did not suffer fools gladly.

My probationary period was rocky. I was still immature during this period of my life and at times somewhat out of my depth, which was reflected in some of my probationary reports. I was reported on several times during my two-year probation.

I can quote some of the comments about me. On my seven-month progress report, dated 1st December 1975:

"He has not got the full hang of police work at present, but this should improve."

"He suffers from lack of confidence."

"He was not getting cooperation from his colleagues too well, and this has brought about a complex, which unsettled him."

After ten months, my reports began to be more positive. Here is a part of progress report, dated 9th February 1976:

"Since my last report, he has improved immensely."

"He brought many problems with him when he joined the Division. At first it appeared that he would not last his two years. With close supervision, there is a gradual improvement."

My thirteen-month -- report was better, dated 14th May 1976:

"He has become more popular with his colleagues."

"It appears that persistent talking to by supervisors has brought this Officer to his senses. He certainly does not lack confidence. Progress has been most pleasing in recent weeks."

My sixteen-month report, dated 10th August 1976 showed more favourable comments. I was now:

"… most popular with my colleagues. He impressed me with his interrogation of persons, says Ron.

These comments were a true appraisal of

me, I certainly did lack confidence, and I was one of the youngest and smallest on the shift. I had taken on the responsibilities of being newly married. Anne had given up on her intended career, and we were both living in a strange place, neither of us having lived outside the West Midlands area before.

Around the end of 1975 Anne was pregnant with our first and only child, and this alone put even more pressure on me. So it was no wonder my early reports reflected the stresses in my life the way they did. My first arrest was on a night duty. I was on foot patrol in the town centre after midnight, and I was walking with Brian, a probationer like me, but a few months ahead of me. Brian lived a few doors down from me, and he was married too. We came across a man lying flat out on the floor, practically unconscious and reeking of booze. We roused him, but he was so obviously drunk, he could not stand on his own, so Brian told me to arrest him for the offence of being drunk and incapable.

We called into the station on our Pye radio, and a van came out to us. We put the bloke in the back and drove him back to the station. A Pye radio was the name of the radio unit, two pieces, one to talk into and the other to listen to, an old antiquated system. It was only a few years before that time that Police Officers still relied on the whistle. In fact, we were still issued with whistles, which formed part of our equipment. I still have mine to this day and I intend to pass it on to my granddaughter. I had to relay to Frank Carsley the grounds for my arrest, and the man was put into a cell to sober up. Then I had to prepare my first ever arrest statement and report.

I experienced my first firearms incident fairly early on. It was on Christmas Day of 1975, and it was domestic-related; and there I was, thinking Christmas Day was a quiet time. It happened somewhere in a residential area, where a man had been to his estranged wife's place and shot her windows out with a shotgun. I was only a small part of this event. The Divisional Commander was called out, Chief Superintendent David Cole. In those days, there were no armed response cars, or any dedicated firearms unit. There were certain Officers known as Authorised Shots, and these were normal patrol Officers who were trained in the use of guns. Authorised shots had been called out, but I can't remember now how many. The bloke had been quickly tracked to a remote house somewhere in the countryside or semi-rural area.

I was the driver for Mr Cole, and I drove him to the scene of the shooting so he could see for himself. I recall an Authorised Shot lying on some grassed area, it may have been a field overlooking the premises where the perpetrator was. The Authorised Shot would be wearing his normal uniform then, not like today where they dress up like Robo Cop. It all ended peacefully with the ex-husband being arrested without anyone getting hurt.

During October and November 1976 I was attached to the Traffic Department at Shrewsbury as. part of my probationary period. The Traffic Officers team back then was a Department of its own. The Officers in this Department were all advanced drivers, and weren't confined to a small area. They were controlled from Headquarters at Worcester and were responsible for the whole of the county of Shropshire. Their type of work was completely different from the work I'd been used to up to then.

For the most part, I was crewed up with a couple of old-timers, George and Neville. They were old enough to be my dad and they usually put me in the back of the car. Needless to say, I was bored because, mainly all we did was drive round country lanes, stopping the odd vehicle for traffic offences. Being controlled by HQ at Hindlip, the Traffic Officer wasn't aware of the Policing jobs in the towns, that was the job of local Divisional personnel and Divisional Controllers. I did not get a favourable report from the Traffic Sergeant. He said that I had an abrasive manner with the driving public, and that I lacked interest. He was not wrong. The only thing I found interesting was at refreshment times when Neville would pull out his magazines from his bag. You know the sort, from the top shelf!! Readers' wives and all that. I had a quick browse through the readers' wives just to see if I knew anyone. Not telling even if I did.

I also did a week in the CID office at Wellington, and this is where I got my first experience of the pranks that were to feature throughout the Service.

Call me gullible if you like, but there was a detective called Andy, who was a comedy character, always liked a joke. On my first morning of my week's CID attachment I entered the office, Andy welcomed me, and there were one or two others in there. He said he'd made some tea and had poured me one, and pointed to a desk in the corner, and duly told me that was the desk I'd be using for the week. Anyway, he invited me to sit at the desk and drink my tea. I sauntered over and placed my backside on the chair at the desk and was just taking a sip of the tea from the cup, when the Detective Sergeant walked into the office, looked at me and said words to the effect, "What the hell do you think you're doing, sat at my desk and drinking my tea?" After that I never trusted anything Andy told me.

I went on to eventually struggle to get through my probationary period, and it was a struggle. I acknowledge that I did have problems. I'm now aware that I was at times abrasive to the public. It is a trait that's always been with me and has been to my detriment. I did not suffer fools gladly, and I particularly did not like people who showed disrespect to the uniform or the Police as an organisation. My problem was blurting things out, or engaging mouth before brain. Fellow officers who didn't know me, but saw me acting this way, well it's fair to say I gave out the wrong impression at times. I owe my career to Ron Gilbert. He took me under his wing and if it hadn't been for him, I would never have got through that two-year period. I also owe a great deal to the new Inspector David. David, I felt, could be a pain to me and at the time, I don't think he liked me particularly, and I disliked his manner and attitude. I acknowledge that what I perceived as his somewhat bully-boy tactics to get me to do things I didn't want to do, did in hind-sight show me that he was determined to get me to be a Policeman in the end. Looking back at those times, I now appreciate he had my best interests at heart.

On September 24th 1976 our son Paul was born at Copthorne Hospital in Shrewsbury. This hospital was about twelve miles from where we lived, and I had no transport, because my Austin 1100 had died and I was not in a financial position to buy another car. Anne had had a false alarm earlier that month and was now two weeks overdue. She went to the hospital on the 23rd September and was kept in, as she had started her labour, which continued for some thirty hours. The day before the birth I was on a two till ten late shift, and due back in at six o'clock in the morning on the day of the birth. I had spoken to Anne on the phone on the 23rd.

Now a few doors up from where we lived was another Officer, Lionel, and his wife. Lionel was a likable character, who was stationed at Oakengates, a small community about 5 miles away from Wellington. He often told his wife he had to work overtime till two in the morning, but in reality he went to Jollies night club in Stoke, then he would go back to the station, don his uniform again and go back home. It's okay to reveal this now, as they got divorced many years ago. Anyway, Lionel had an old clapped-out mini, and on the day of Paul's birth, I had a phone call from the hospital to say that Anne was being taken to theatre to have a Caesarean. My Sergeant allowed me to finish, but I had no transport, and Lionel very kindly allowed me to use his car. It was parked in the town, where his wife worked, and I went to collect the key from her.

It was raining and I had got halfway to the hospital when the windscreen wipers packed up, and I had to stick my head out of the window to see where I was going. When I got there, Paul had already been born and Anne was back in her hospital bed, still sedated from the anaesthetic. Looking through a screen, I saw our son in his crib in a large room alongside other babies. I had to check with the nurses, to make sure it was my son. I wouldn't want to have taken the wrong one home. This was another proud moment for me. Only a few years before, in fact six years before, I had been in front of a magistrate. In that six years, I had achieved being accepted into the Police, got married and became a father, and I was growing up rapidly.

CHAPTER FOUR
TRANSFER TO REDDITCH

I spent two years completing my probationary period at Wellington. I learned a lot, and there wasn't much going on in the way of pranks; and initiation stuff? That didn't seem to happen. Well, not for me in any case.

I do remember there was a close bond with the Ministry of Defence. There was a large MOD base at Donnington, an area outside Wellington, but which was part of the Wellington Sub-Division. A couple of times a year they would hold social events where the Police were invited, and it was at one of these events, in late 1975, that Anne fainted, and she was attended to by an army medic. He enquired if she was pregnant and of course she said no.

He told us that it was often a sign of pregnancy. How right he was, she was pregnant, but didn't know it at the time.

There was one other young officer on the Sub-Division. I can't remember his name, he was always throwing some sort of party. We attended one of his parties one evening, a fancy dress party. I can't remember the theme, but he had party prizes to give away. To qualify for a prize, we all had to run around the town. I think it may have been Oakengates, and we had to basically run around dressed like idiots, and we were tanked up with booze, enjoying ourselves, making a right racket around the neighborhood late at night. Luckily the local Police weren't called, or at least I don't think they were.

My appointment as a fully-fledged Constable was eventually confirmed in June 1977. With that hurdle out of the way, I needed to get back near to our home town. Redditch was my goal. I needed a cunning plan to persuade the Superintendent to grant a transfer to the new town. It was no use my telling him I was homesick, or that I didn't like it at Telford. The truth was that Anne was eager to get back nearer to home. What with a young baby and all that, our life would be easier nearer to family. We had no transport and relied on her father to come to Wellington to take us back and forth. Anne's mother, Mary, suffered from multiple sclerosis. Although not confined to a wheelchair at that time, she did need a stick to get about. (Her condition later deteriorated to a point where she was practically bedridden at the end of her life and had to have a leg amputated.) With the blessing of Anne, I compiled a report to the Sub-Divisional Superintendent. I explained all about how Mary needed her daughter to be nearer home, and how Anne would visit and help look after her. I must add that we had the blessing of Anne's parents.

In the summer of 1977, my transfer request was granted and I was posted to Redditch. I had to make my own removal arrangements. Bill, a neighbour and fellow officer, helped me pack a hired van, and allowed Anne and me to sleep the night at his Police house two doors away. A few trips to Redditch had to be made to sort out accommodation. Redditch, like Telford, was a new town, and a lot of new housing was being built there.

Unfortunately, there was a shortage of Police houses, but I was given two addresses to view. Both houses were brand new and the Police were going to rent them from the Redditch New Town Development Corporation. The housing stock was later transferred to the local Authority. We opted for 233 Loxley Close, Church Hill, Redditch. The housing in the Close was brand new and there was building work still going on around the place. Most of the new tenants were young couples in the same boat as us, with one of them working. We soon got to know the neighbours and they seemed okay with the fact that I was a Police Officer. Over the years the rules were relaxed, and outsiders began moving into the houses, and, not to disrespect today's residents in the area, like many similar estates around the country, it soon became a place of increasing crime, and it began attracting undesirables.

The local pub, the Book and Candle, became a place where drug deals were done, and it was raided on occasions. The shopping centre next door to the pub attracted gangs of youths and petty crime, and elderly folk wouldn't go there at night to shop. Today all that has gone including the pub, which has been redeveloped with new houses.

These new properties were crammed in and of a modern terrace type, partly centrally heated, this on the lower floor only. It was a three-bedroomed property with a small garden and a low wired fence at the rear, separating the properties, so everyone could see across to other gardens. The other residents occupying the properties were mostly people from the Birmingham overspill area. I was aware that other Police Officers were strewn across various parts of the New Town, also in rented properties.

The number of Police personnel was on the increase in the town, due to the large influx of new people, and the expanding conurbation. In those days, Redditch Police Station was in Church Road in the town centre, but there was a new modern police station being constructed in Grove Street, also in the town, as the Church Road premises were antiquated and not fit for the purpose.

The new Police Station was state of the art in its day, when it became the Divisional Headquarters, with six modern male cells, two female cells and two juvenile cells; it also had a medical room, and a prisoner entrance with electric gates to the yard that led to the cell block. On the top floor were several single men's bedrooms, with a communal lounge and eating area. We are talking 1979, so not that long ago in terms of buildings. Today the cell block does not meet the current standards, and has been shut down, the management has moved to other Police stations, and the public counter is now only part time. In short, it is a half-condemned concrete box now. The old Police Station only housed 4 cells, and it was adjacent to the magistrates' court. This, too, was for the chop, as a new court complex was also being constructed next door to the new station, with a tunnel from the cell block to the docks in the court.

We moved into our new home, which Anne was not happy with, and to some extent neither was I, but I was in a disciplined service and I had no choice. I arrived at Redditch Station to join my new shift. My old class mate, Dick was on that shift, and it was good to be seeing him again.

There were two Sergeants on my shift, one of whom was John. He had been a Constable on my shift at Wellington back in 1975, before he was promoted to Redditch some eight months or so before I transferred. He was a tall man, with a dry sense of humour, who spoke in a quiet manner, and not much seemed to faze him. Another Sergeant was Terry. He was completely different, smaller and thicker set than John. I found that he could be abrasive at times, but he had lots of confidence, and was supportive of his shift. The shift Inspector was Roger. He had thick grey hair, but he was younger than he looked, and he was known as the Silver Fox. He was not the most popular Inspector at the station, because he was a disciplinarian, and a stickler for pocket book rules.

Every Police Officer is issued with a pocket book. These are numbered and a record kept at central admin. We were expected to make an entry every hour or so of what we were doing and our location, and any events or offences had to be recorded. If we were to report any offences on the street, such as a bald tyre on a car, for example, the reference number relating to that offence had to be listed against the pocket book entry. This pocket book procedure was not uniform across the Division, it was a Roger requirement, and what Roger wanted, Roger got. In fact, anything we dealt with had to be recorded somewhere, in the General Occurrence Book (GOB), for example. This book would be used for non-crime stuff, such as a road accidents involving dogs (back then, all such accidents had, by law, to be reported to the Police), or rubbish fires, where Police attended.

A Process book was used for listing a person's details and for offences reported, such as traffic offences. A Minor Complaint Book was used for complaints such as kids playing football in the street, or minor vandalism, and then there was the Crime Reporting Register, where crime numbers were generated. Each entry into any of these books had to have a reference number and the Inspector insisted that the reference number also be inserted alongside the incident in our pocket book. Later, West Mercia continued to develop their computer systems, and all these books and registers would disappear in favour of the digital age.

At any time during a shift, either the Patrol Sergeant or the Inspector might meet us on the street and examine our book, and sometimes we had to write it up to date while they waited, and then they would sign it. Sometimes they might say, "Leave me a line." This would mean leaving a space, and recording the time of the meeting on the street with the Sergeant and they would later sign it before going off duty. At going-off-duty time we all had to queue up outside the Inspector's office and one by one we would go in, and he would look through our pocket book, and if we had missed any reference numbers, we had to go back and find it and re-join the queue.

I sometimes did not get home till late,

after having my book examined, which took place all in our own time, I might add.

Apparently, none of the other shift Inspectors were that meticulous. Rumour had it that our shift Inspector had been disciplined some time over a pocket book matter, but this was just a rumour and may have been false. Another Officer on the shift was George; older than me by about 10 years, he was from the south of the country, a generally likeable and jovial man who was always smiling. He was tall, slim, and had long legs that bowed slightly, he loved sport and was a keep fit fanatic. He was always sharing a joke and sometimes annoyed Roger, the shift Inspector. He was the sort of person who had tea stops across the town, and I remember one event when we were part of a regional PSU (Police Support Unit), with other Forces, for a demonstration in West Bromwich. The right wing group The National Front were holding a meeting and anti-fascist protesters were supposed to be turning up.

The National Front was a right-wing group of idiots and thugs, not to put a finer point on it. Today you can liken them to the English Defence League and similar groups, who spout on about the same stuff the National Front did, and of course social media was not about in those days to stoke things up either, in the way that organisations do, like Britain First, which is loosely a social media right-wing group. We weren't dressed in riot gear in those days; in fact it was not until the late eighties that shields were introduced, and then the helmets around the time of the miners' strike (more on that later). Our unit was posted on the street outside a school. George, in his wisdom, left the ranks and headed into the school, to return with a tray full of cups of tea. That was George for you, a cheeky but likeable character.

I remember one particular morning, when we were out in the rear yard, cleaning and generally checking over the Police cars. Inspector Harris had the bonnet up on the Inspector's car, and George was inside, attempting to get it started, while the Inspector was looking under the bonnet to try and see what the problem might be. I was cleaning a car nearby, and Inspector Harris popped his head above the bonnet and called to George not to start the engine. "Okay," replied George and then began to attempt to start the engine, just as the Inspector was holding the fan belt. Well, his fingers were taken on a ride around the fan belt spool, with the Inspector shouting profanities at George. Luckily, he was not badly injured, just a few sore fingers. George responded, "I misheard you. I thought you said, 'start the engine.'" How we all laughed quietly to ourselves on that occasion.

In all, there were about ten Constables on the shift, a lot in those days. Redditch town had a couple of night clubs, and in the centre at weekends there was a hotdog stand, where crowds used to gather in the early hours when the clubs turned out. It was a hotspot for fights, and prior to my transfer to the town, there had been a large fight and Officers were injured. On that occasion, one shift of Officers were ambushed at the hot dog stand by a group of people who hated the Police. This resulted in a crown court trial, and some of those found guilty ended up with prison sentences. Of course, if this were today, these places that attracted trouble would be closed down. I never experienced anything like this, I am glad to say, although I witnessed plenty of fights and drunkenness, and Friday and Saturday nights always meant that our four cells at the old station were full. Each cell had a toilet, which was not concealed, so there was no privacy for anyone occupying a cell.

It was usual in those days to house more than one person to a cell, and I have known as many as eight.

There would be all sorts of questions asked today if more than one person were put in a cell. Before I retired, it was normal for Custody Sergeants to shut the custody suite when the cell accommodation was full. Yet back then it wasn't deemed to be a problem. If the cells were full, any prisoners had to be transported to the next available cell space, and if there weren't any, well, they had to either be released or queue until a cell was free.

The Human Rights Act had a lot to do with these decisions. In fact, the Human Rights Act was one piece of legislation that altered many aspects of Policing. That's not to say that we were inhumane in our treatment of people at all!

The Police Service was brought under the umbrella of another new piece of Legislation, that of Health and Safety, and this had a huge impact on the functions of the

Police. Before the service was bound by the Health and Safety regulations, it was not unusual for Policing methods to be high risk. For example, once we had a spate of burglaries on a factory Estate in Redditch, which were being discovered by factory staff in the mornings. So, we had to organise observation posts throughout the night. One set of nights, I had to sit inside a factory on my own all night in case criminals broke in, and I was expected to shout out for help if they did. I can tell you it was pretty scary, sitting there in a dark, large, open factory, with every little noise setting your mind off, imagining all sorts of things.

It wasn't just factories, it also involved building sites. Redditch was a fast-developing town and there were building sites aplenty, which brought with it a high proportion of thefts, and I don't mean just bags of sand and a few bricks. Sometimes almost completed houses had bathrooms, or kitchens removed. Later, the new legislation introduced the risk assessment regime and any operation which involved observations, or raids on premises, even planned road checks, had to be risked assessed, and had be signed off; another tier of bureaucracy, and some would say for the better. Once the new legislation came about, it was very rare to see this type of Policing. Certainly, a lone Officer wouldn't – or shouldn't – be put in a vulnerable position again, which I suppose is a good thing, although I'm reliably informed that it's not uncommon for relatively new Officers to have to work night shifts alone, despite policies supposedly preventing it.

I recall a disturbance on the new town which happened one night. Alison, one of the Policewomen on the shift, had been punched in the face by a couple of men, the shift responded and two men were arrested. The cell passage was quite narrow, and had piping work just below the ceiling. The cells went off to the left, next to each other. Prisoners were taken into the Sergeant's office, next door to the small radio room, which usually had one PC and a civilian operator in those days. Tony was the Duty Constable working in the control room. Tony was a large-built man, some might say he was overweight. One of the men who assaulted Alison was carried into the Sergeant's Office, struggling and fighting and being generally abusive. We managed to get him onto the floor, but we were having problems keeping him down.

Despite what you see on the television, Police dramas where one officer easily brings a violent person under control, it's not like that in real life. Suddenly the door to the radio room swung open, and in the doorway to the Sergeant's office was Tony, his bulk filling the whole space. The only thing that was missing was a batman cape and mask. Tony charged across the room and sort of launched himself off the ground and landed with his full weight on the prisoner, winding him and making him easier to control. There was none of this namby-pamby stuff of today, with restraint controls or protective clothing, just a bit of good old fashion roughness to get the job sorted. Nowadays it's all wrist locks, arm bars, pepper spray, tasers and other stuff that people can't remember from one yearly training course to another - back then it was basically a scrap.

The prisoner was dragged, screaming and kicking to a cell, where we locked him in. Immediately, he started banging on and kicking the door, inviting us all in for a fight. He had a bad case of acne, and some of his spots had burst and he had traces of blood on his face. To a layperson, it may have appeared he had been assaulted but this was not the case. So, having placed him in a cell, we brought his mate into the station. He was calmer, but could hear his pal shouting from the cell, making accusations that we had given him a good pasting, and warning him to be careful. The second chap was more compliant and we put him in a cell next door. The mouthy one continued shouting abuse, when suddenly there was an almighty crash coming from within the cell. The prisoner had somehow smashed the toilet, and was now holding a long, sharp, pointed piece of porcelain.

He invited us in to take it off him. The Sergeants decided no one was going to go in. These were the days before the riot shield, or protective helmets. The Sergeants decided there was only one person to do the job, and that was PC Frank Roberts and his partner. Frank was the duty dog handler and his partner was the dog, who was somewhere out on the patch. I don't recall the dog's name, but it was a German Shepherd, as most Police dogs were. Frank was an experienced dog handler, having also served as one in the RAF. He was a scouser and a very popular man who revelled in dealing with this type of situation, and with idiots like the one in the cell. Frank was called in and arrived in the cell passage with his German shepherd Police dog.

Frank moved us all back and began to wind the dog up. The prisoner was shouting, and Frank was talking to the dog, saying,

"Who is it? Go on, what's he doing? Go on, where is he then?" The dog's barking was getting louder, and he was salivating at the mouth, the prisoner still behind the safety of his door, still goading the officers and holding the piece of porcelain. As soon as Frank had finished preparing his dog for the grand opening of the cell door, the prisoner was given one last warning to drop the weapon, but he continued to invite us in for a spot of tiffin, so to speak.

So, without further ado, the cell door was unlocked and it swung open. Confronting the prisoner was now a large ferocious dog, foaming at the mouth and showing the him his nice, clean, sharp fangs, and barking incessantly at him, the prisoner still holding the porcelain piece. Frank had him on a short leash, using the strength of his arm to hold the dog back, the dog's two front legs off the floor, and his back legs moving at a heck of a rate, trying to free itself from Frank's grip. A look of terror and horror swept across the prisoner's face, and he quickly dropped the weapon and cowered in the corner, squealing like a small child. The dog was kept on the lead and did not get to taste his quarry, although I like to think he could smell his fear. The prisoner was removed to the passageway and he was handcuffed to one of the overhead pipes until he had calmed down. Unfortunately, alcohol had played a contributing role. He was later charged with assault on Police and criminal damage to the cell. I don't know what the outcome of this case was. All through the Policing process, we start and deal with cases, but once they're handed over to the court system, it's not often that we get to hear the end result, unless it's a not guilty plea and we're in the court to hear the result.

I continued working on this shift as a patrol Officer, doing the day-to-day normal Policing. I would sometimes be working as a panda driver and other days I would be walking the town. Whoever was on the town beat on nights was expected to check all property thoroughly, shaking hands with door handles of the retail premises, and getting to the rear of the premises, and even checking flat roofs. A PC called Andy, if my memory serves me correctly, was the night town walker one evening, though he was not on my shift. We had only shortly before this moved from Church Road to the new station at Grove Street.

The old police station and court complex was closed up, but not yet demolished. Opposite the old Police station was a large building which was a bingo club. One morning the staff discovered that someone had broken into the club, and stolen a large amount of property, including bottles of booze. This was discovered at about eight o'clock in the morning. The stolen property was found across the road in the old Police station. Poor Andy was called out of bed, having only just gone off duty a few hours before. He had to report to the Superintendent and explain why he had not discovered this crime. Oh, how I miss the good old days (not).

This type of thing faded out as the years went on, perhaps the Human Rights Act, or Health and Safety played a part in it, or perhaps the Police Service, as a whole was just becoming less regimented, less disciplined, and certainly back then you didn't question the reasons; if a person of rank said jump, then your only acceptable response would be to enquire as to the required height of said jump. Not like towards the end of my service, when junior ranks would question decisions, or even refuse to carry out a lawful instruction. A grievance procedure was later introduced, so if there was any conflict between supervisors and the lower ranks, all sorts of procedures had to be gone through. I dare say there have even been numerous allegations of bullying, when an Officer was required to carry out his or her duty, but didn't feel like it. This helped in some ways, but it never stopped the ambitious ones, who would shit on anyone just to get to where they wanted to go.

CID looked into the crime at the bingo club, and it transpired that it had a connection to a member of the Police. A fairly recent recruit, a Policewoman, who was, as I recall, still in her probationary period, had started having a relationship with a miscreant from the Batchley area of the town. With her knowledge and his criminal background, he burgled the place and stashed the stolen goods in the old Police Station. She was in on it, and both were subsequently arrested and charged. She was sacked and the two of them continued living in the town. She and her boyfriend featured in the local paper some time later, as they had been evicted from their rented home, and were reported to be living in a car. This incident was not the only one to bring about the downfall of Police Officers in Redditch.

When I first arrived in Redditch there were three incidents on the go, all happening just prior to my arrival. I didn't know those involved personally and I never met them. There were two CID officers suspended on my arrival. Apparently they had seized some items of some description but had not listed them. I seem to recall it might have been booze that they'd drunk. It was a daft and silly thing to do, and a sure way of ending what could have been a very good career. In another incident, a village beat Officer was suspended. Their patch was a small village on the outskirts of Redditch that had its own Police house with an office and the beat Officer lived and worked from there. It transpired that locals were going away on holiday and returning to find their homes had been burgled. The unnamed beat Officer was charged with these offences. The victims had told him that they were going away, and in doing that, they'd given him almost an invitation to break into their houses, and some property, I believe, was found in the loft at the Police house where he lived.

Then there was the case of another Policewoman. Again I will not say her real name, but for the purpose of this tale I will call her Gail. Gail was well-liked and was from the north-west area of the UK, with the accent that goes with it. She'd been on CID attachment at times, as well as being the Divisional Drugs Liaison Officer. She was known to be gay, and in those days, being gay was not something you talked freely about, certainly not in the Police Service. Of course, today things have improved for the better. She was well thought of as a dedicated and efficient Officer. Gail had become involved in the dealings of a persistent female shoplifter from the new town area. Gail was involved in processing this shoplifter and interviewing her. The two of them formed a relationship, which Gail had kept secret. The bond between them was strong, so much so that Gail was suspected by some at the time of in some way either covering up her crimes, or of being some sort of an accomplice to them.

Gail ended up being arrested herself, and she subsequently lost her job. It went further than this, though, and Gail would see the inside of a cell on more than one occasion, as the relationship between her and her friend soured and turned nasty. Gail badly assaulted her friend and ended up on a serious assault charge. I can't remember what happened to her after that. It saddens me to see people with such good prospects throw them away like that. I suppose people we consider "bad apples" turn up in all walks of life, but when it's the Police Service, it affects all good hard-working Officers, and puts the reputation of the Service in a bad light, giving its critics fuel to further lambast us.

Of course, being a victim of crime could happen to anyone. It happened to me and my family in 1978 in Weymouth in Dorset. The incident sent shudders down my spine. My Mother always went to Weymouth for her yearly holiday, and back in those days, money was tight and we couldn't afford expensive hotels. My Mother put me in touch with a bed and breakfast in Weymouth, apparently associated with the people who ran a bed and breakfast where she was staying. I booked it, and when we arrived, it looked pretty much like the rest of the places on the beach front, and had the usual signs in the windows showing either vacancies or no vacancies. Our room was on an upper floor with a couple of rooms opposite. It had a double bed and a temporary bed for our son Paul, who at the time was only 2 years old. There were no en suites in those days, and there was a communal bathroom on the floor our room was on. We went down for breakfast the next morning, expecting perhaps to see other families, and we did see other guests, but most were single people, some sitting together, chatting. A mixture of men and women, not very old. We thought nothing of this and we spent the day out on the beach, pushing Paul around in his push chair.

As I said, money was tight, and I only had about twenty pounds cash, and Anne had a couple of notes in her purse

We both smoked cigarettes in those days. Before dinner Anne wanted to rest, so she lay on the bed and I took Paul out in his pushchair and arrived back an hour or so later. Anne woke up and we went for our evening meal, and then went out again, I think to visit the local funfair. While we were out, Anne discovered money missing from her purse, and at first she thought I'd taken it. She also noticed some of her cigarettes were missing. We came to the conclusion that the money had been stolen from our room. We went back to the B&B, and we turned our room upside down. The lock on the room was the kind you needed a key for, and when I took Paul out to leave Anne to rest, I didn't lock the door. The person in the room opposite ours was a man, a dodgy looking bloke, and my instincts told me I couldn't not trust him as far as I could throw him. I started to wonder then why there were no other families in the place. I went and spoke to the owner and told her that money and cigarettes had gone missing and I suspected someone had been in our room while Anne was asleep.

I told her that I was a serving Police

Officer, and she said that most of her guests were placed there by Social Services, and that the man opposite our room had been released from prison just two days before. That was it, the local Police were informed and within half an hour we'd packed our cases and left the B&B. We were effectively without any accommodation then, and we trawled the seafront looking for an affordable hotel. We managed to find a hotel, but could only afford a few days. The local Police came to see us, and the man in the room opposite ours was arrested and interviewed. He'd been in prison before for burglary, and confessed straight away, admitting he'd entered our room while Anne was asleep and rifled her handbag.

He was charged and put before the court the next day and sentenced to one month in prison. That'll teach him - not. I was thankful Anne hadn't woken up at the time, as I shudder to think what he would have done.

CHAPTER FIVE
NEW STATION

In 1978 we, the Police, moved from Church Road into the new station at Grove Street. It was a modern four-storey building. The top floor comprised two canteens; one was a small area for senior Officers, and the other was for the rest of us. Anyone above the rank of Sergeant was a senior Officer. There were a number of single men's bedrooms and a single men's lounge. There was a new Police Club with a bar, dance floor and snooker room; a dedicated control room, and a brand new cell block, giving us ten cells, six for men, two for women, and two juvenile detention rooms. The cell block had a doctor's room, and a holding area for prisoners waiting to be processed, as well as an exercise yard.

At the time of writing this, the cell block is closed as being unfit for purpose, but back then it was the "bee's knees."

The building had been planned in the late sixties, and on the plans, there was a Policewomen's department office. Of course, in 1974 when the Police Forces amalgamated, the

Policewomen's department had been done away with and Policewomen had become formerly recognised as equal to their male counterparts. To think, this archaic procedure was still in place only a few years ago and was seen as totally normal. Over the years there were many alterations to the inside of the building, partitions put up in large open spaces to make more office space, the control room moved twice from the ground floor onto the second floor, then ending up on the top floor, before eventually being swallowed by a Forcewide communications room at Headquarters. The single men's bedrooms were altered, some removed to make bigger offices and the others to become extra offices. Then they even closed the club room down and made that into an office too. (I always said that if I ever became Chief Constable the first thing I would do is reintroduce the Club and the snooker table).

The rear of the building that backs onto the car park was a large garage area with a number of metal sliding doors, and this garage area became the new home for Officers' lockers. The building was a square shape and had a suspended garden on the first floor in the central hub of the building. (the suspended garden was removed after a few years and a suspended new floor and offices replaced it). The space below the garden was the cell entrance area, with room for parking for about half a dozen Police vehicles. There was an automated shutter door at the access to the parking area, controlled by a button in the control room.

The rule was that all cars parking in this space under the garden had to be reversed in. There was a downward ramp through the shutter doors. One day sometime possibly in the late seventies, maybe the early eighties, I was driving one of the two Morris Marina Divisional cars. These were initially plain cars, unmarked, but when Mr Cozens became Chief Constable, a Police sticker was put on the sides. I had positioned the car to reverse back, I put it in neutral and freewheeled back on the slope towards the brick wall, next to the door to the charge office in the custody block. As I got near the wall, I braked, or so I thought, but my foot was hovering over the clutch. I panicked and before I had chance to move my foot to the brake, the rear end smashed into the brickwork beside that door into the custody block.

From the rolling position at the start, the distance was a good fifteen metres, and I can tell you, the speed soon built up, and I probably hit the wall at about ten miles per hour, and I know this doesn't sound fast, but it gave me a jolt. Apparently, the people on the other side of the cell entrance door felt a shake, and it was loud enough to catch the attention of others in the building. The left side of the rear of the car was crumpled up, and the door to the custody bock swung open, and another door to the main station just to the right flung open, and there I was, confronted by a load of Officers having a good laugh at my expense. I felt a right Charlie, because not only had I smashed up one of the most popular and much-used cars, I knew there would be consequences.

The Duty Sergeant was not best pleased in having to deal with this incident. I was immediately suspended from driving Police cars (The consequence) and was not allowed to drive again until I passed another Police driving test, which I had to do six months later, and which, fortunately, I passed with flying colours. I spent the next six months pounding the beat on foot.

I continued in general Policing duties at the new station, and it was really quite different, as the new station housed a lot of gaffers. While we were at the old Police Station, the senior command team had been housed in rented office space in the Kingfisher Shopping Centre. In the new station, the Divisional Commander was based there, his deputy a Superintendent, and both these people were on the top floor. The Division in those days consisted of the towns of Redditch and Bromsgrove. There were two Sub-Divisions, one was Redditch and the other Bromsgrove. Redditch Sub-Division comprised Redditch, Wythall, Alvechurch, and out as far as Inkeberrow. Bromsgrove consisted of Bromsgrove, Rubery, Frankley, and at various times Droitwich and Hagley. (Over the years these two towns were passed between Kidderminster and Worcester Divisions.)

On the floor below the Chief Superintendent, was the Sub-Division Commander and his assistant, responsible for the day to day Policing operations in Redditch. These were a Superintendent and a Chief

Inspector. Bromsgrove Police station also had the same structure. During my time at the new station, or in Redditch generally, different gaffers came and went, either by retiring or by using the position as a stepping stone onto bigger things.

Some of the gaffers were good and well respected, others could be abrasive and a bit up themselves.

One particular Chief Superintendent that came along was a man who had previously served in another Force. He had a moustache, and was medium build and well-groomed, but small in height; in fact, I don't know how he ever became a Police Officer. He must have been five feet, seven inches at the most. He was a man not to upset, and in my eyes at least, he looked upon the lower ranks as those who needed to know their place. That was how I perceived him, anyway, though I may have been wrong, but I am sure he was probably a man who looked upon his role as that of a leader. After all, he got to where he was, I am sure for his attributes.

He did not suffer fools gladly and he was

treated with caution by a lot of the staff below him, most certainly by junior ranked Police Officers.

His office overlooked the junction of Archer Street and Grove Street, and on the corner there was a café, and there were double yellow lines around the junction.

On Evesham Road at Headless Cross in the old part of town was a small two-storey apartment block, where his mother lived. There were no such double yellow lines outside her address. All of this becomes relevant in a moment! Every morning at nine o'clock, the Duty Sergeant had to be available with the previous day's events, reported crimes, prisoner numbers, telephone logs, and any other daily records. The Chief Superintendent and/or his Deputy would go through the documents in great detail. The Duty Sergeant was expected to have the answer to any queries and to know about any progress being made on these enquiries; in short, it was a daily briefing, but an extensive one for the Chief Superintendent and his Deputies.

During the early 1980s from about 1985

to my promotion in 1989, I worked as a Controller on and off in the operations room, this being during the reign of this Chief Superintendent. He was forever ringing down to the control room if he saw a vehicle parked on double lines outside the café, and he would instruct me to have an Officer place a parking ticket on it, and to present the counterfoil of the parking ticket to him. If I told him there was no one on the shift to do it because they were busy, he would tell me there were plenty of office-bound Officers within the Station and to get one of them to do it. On many occasions, I felt like telling him to get off his fat arse and do it himself.

Every Saturday morning the Duty Sergeant had to make sure a couple of no-waiting cones were placed on Evesham Road outside his mother's address by nine o'clock in the morning. This was because his mother (so rumour had it) did not like the general motoring public parking outside her address. He would often phone in if the cones weren't in place. On one occasion, Superintendent Poulton, (now deceased) who was once the Sub-Divisional Commander, phoned into the control room while he was out shopping with his wife around the town, wanting to know who the town beat Officer was, and why he could not see him or her around the town. I thought to myself,

"Hang on, Sir. I'll just go and consult my crystal bloody ball, shall I?" I probably called up the town beat Constable to ask who he or she was.

The Controller role was supposed to be that of controlling the Sub-Division, dispatching Officers to jobs, yet those who were not a Controller, or not familiar with the role, thought you were some sort of super genius who had all the answers as to who was where, or what was what.

Now, I am going to tell you about a very serious and traumatic incident that occurred in the Police Station during the watch of this Chief Superintendent. Now, if any of you reading this is of a nervous disposition, stop reading now. Just thinking about it as I write is sending shivers down my spine.

The incident occurred in the Police Club at Redditch, but I don't have the dates. It was probably the most serious thing to happen in all the Police Force. It was a case that baffled the mind of the Detective Chief Inspector and his

Deputy, the Detective Inspector who was tasked with dealing with it. What could it possibly be? I hear you ask. Well, some miscreant member of staff had drawn a false moustache and a pair of glasses on the Chief Constable's portrait in the clubroom. This dastardly crime was one notch below that of murder. All hell broke loose and the Chief Superintendent was not amused. I can just picture him now when he found out about it. Steam coming from his ears, jumping up and down on the floor behind his desk, the top of his head appearing above the line of the top of his desk, his Deputies standing there, saying nothing, listening to him ranting. Okay, I may be exaggerating a little, and he was small but not that small. Sorry, Sir but the image I had was funny. The Divisional Detective Inspector was tasked to investigate and to bring the miscreant before the boss.

Each shift was visited at their parades and told that this was a joke until some set date, and then it would become a crime recording matter.

Over the coming weeks, numerous people were interviewed and eliminated. I was not even in the Club at the time, so I was innocent. The matter slowly died a death, as no one was ever identified, although there was a name being bandied about the Station. That named person was interviewed and never confessed.

There are things that happen in a person's lifetime that you just don't forget, that always stay with you, and this incident is one of them. This wouldn't happen in today's Police Service. In those days, people holding a high rank were seen as God and you did not question their instructions.

One particular day there was an animal rights demonstration at Becketts Farm on the A435 at Wythall, an outpost in the north of the Division. Becketts Farm is still about today, but back then it was mainly a small bakery and provisions store, and they housed battery hens, and were egg producers amongst other things.

The Animal Rights movement was very active in those days, and along with sheep farmers, producers of battery eggs were targets of the Animal Rights Liberation Group. These were people mainly from the political left, agitators looking for an excuse to battle those in authority. They had a history of disruption, and a little violence, and an agenda of making complaints against the Police. One tactic they used was to goad Officers into a reaction, while other members of their group made video recordings. On this particular day, intelligence suggested that they were going to arrive en masse at Becketts to demonstrate about the battery hens. Police Support Units were arriving at the site, from around the Force.

Police Officers lined the hedgerow alongside the main A435 dual carriageway. There was an air of tension as the demonstrators began to gather further down the road, because there was no way they would be allowed onto the Becketts car park or land. Now, the Chief Superintendent, the same one as the Picture Gate incident, was due to attend, and we were told he was on his way.

There was a hedge surrounding the farm, bordering with the main A435 dual carriageway, and this hedge stood about four feet high. I was with the Commander of the Special Constables, a man named John Lewis. Not only was John the Division's Special

Constabulary Commander, he was also employed as the Divisional driver handyman. John was a lovable, kind, gentle man, he lived for the Police Service. During the day he did his day job around the Division, and at weekends he was either walking the beat as a Special Constable, or manning one of the public order vans. John was famous for his handlebar moustache. Because John held the rank of Special Commander, his uniform had all the emblems of a Chief, including a flat cap with braiding on the peak and he wore brown gloves. To the general public, he would be seen as a senior Police Officer. I told John to give me his flat Police Cap and his brown gloves.

I carefully placed the hat on the top of the hedge and carefully placed a glove perched on the hedge either side of the hat. I then shouted out to all that the boss had arrived and pointed to the hat and gloves laid precariously on top of the hedge. From a distance, it looked as if his head was just below the hedge line with his hands holding the top of the hedge in an attempt to peer over the top. Everyone thought that was funny. He soon arrived and I quickly removed the evidence before I sparked the

Hedge Gate enquiry. This happened some 30 years ago, and John Lewis died recently. Someone I know went to see John in hospital a week before he died, and he relayed this story to him, and I was told he lay there on his deathbed, chuckling to himself.

The Chief Superintendent was eventually replaced by another, and this was normal practice, it could have been a career move or for other reasons, but it's not unusual for the top brass to get moved around. He was moved shortly after the tragic and sudden death of a serving officer. The officer was a Constable who had committed suicide by shooting himself with a shotgun. The whole incident was unpleasant, and upsetting. The Chief Superintendent is ultimately responsible for the good order of his Division, including integrity and discipline, and this is the same for any leader of men, not just this Chief Superintendent. It was just unfortunate that this event happened on his watch. Now, I don't have any knowledge of whether he had anything to do with the decisions made, or if those decisions were made by others, in the big house at Hindlip (HQ), for example. I do not cast any aspersions on anyone here. It is for the reader to draw his or her own conclusions about whether or not things could have been dealt with differently. Hindsight is a wonderful thing.

For the purpose of this event, I will call the Constable John, not his real name. The time was in the mid- eighties, and I was performing the role of acting Sergeant, having been successful in my promotion exam. I had not yet been on a promotion board, but I was being groomed, so to speak. I was on A shift, (the shift lettering system having gone full circle; nowadays and, you guessed it, this has been branded as a new idea) and a friend from my days at Wellington was the Substantial Sergeant. There was one other, whose name escapes me, and the Inspector was actually a Sergeant who was acting in the role of Inspector. The Acting Inspector and I were car-sharing, taking it in turns to drive each other to work, as we lived near each other.

We had been on six am till two pm early shift and were due back the next day. I learned there had been a meeting that morning with the gaffers about John. John was married to a woman who had been married before, and had a couple of young children. John's father was a magistrate, as I recall somewhere in Shropshire. John was a likable character, a placid, quiet man, who wouldn't say a bad word to anyone.

It turned out that John had been stopped on suspicion of shoplifting by some shop staff shortly before this in a shop in the town centre, while off duty. I wasn't privy to any information about when exactly this happened, whether it was days or even weeks before. I don't even know if he was reported by the store, all I know is that this information was fed back to those of rank. There may be someone out there today who knows more than me, but Police Officers are members of the public and are innocent until proven guilty.

As I recall, the item that was alleged to have been involved was a lamp for a pedal cycle. In the station confines were a number of pedal cycles, which were for use by beat Officers, not that they were ever used. It was said that a lamp from one of these cycles was missing, and the handyman who was responsible for the maintenance of the bikes reported this missing lamp. I don't think there was any assumption that John was involved. Someone of rank, whether it had been instigated in-house on Division, or made by someone at HQ, had decided that an appointed senior detective, who I believe was the station Detective Inspector, would start an investigation. Now, I don't know if a warrant had been applied for or not, I am not in a position to say. I learned that John's house would be visited later that afternoon and that they would be speaking to him. There was also talk of his home being searched as well.

The next morning at around quarter to six, the Acting Inspector and I arrived in the rear yard at Redditch ready for the day's shift, and as we were going in the back door, we were met by one of our shift Constables, Graham Mitchell, who was just on his way out. (Graham was a popular character who went on to become a Detective Sergeant, and he sadly passed away recently)

"Where are you going?" I asked him. He gave me the address he was going to.

"That's John's house," I said.

"Yes, it is. I hate to be the one to tell you,

but John's dead. He shot himself yesterday afternoon at home." What a bombshell. It came as a complete shock to the both of us. Graham told us John's home had been searched the afternoon before. I don't know to this day if anything was found. After the search, he apparently told his wife that they (meaning the job) had got their claws into him and would not let go. With that he went into an upstairs room and shot himself. How awful for his family. The incident reverberated around the Force, and I understand his father made a complaint to the Police.

John's funeral was attended by a large crowd, and he had a full Police send-off, with his hearse being escorted by motor cycle outriders. He is laid to rest at Redditch Crematorium. I've visited his grave stone, it has a pair of handcuffs, if I recall correctly, embossed onto the stone. I do not know the full story surrounding this event, all I do know is that it was a tragic loss of a young life. Who knows what was going on in John's life? He may have had financial problems, he may have been suffering from depression, or stress, a man too proud to seek help, but whatever the truth of it all, he did not deserve to end his life the way he did.

Not long after this event, the Chief Superintendent was replaced as the Divisional Commander. Change of command is not unusual at any time. It may have been as a result if this event, it may not. As I said, I am making no assumptions. It was just as tragic for the Command Team that something like this should happen during their watch. Once again, hindsight is a wonderful thing. It was a sign of the times in those days. The Chief Superintendent went into retirement; I have seen him a couple of times at dinners held by the West Mercia National Association of Retired Police Officers. I haven't spoken to him and I very much doubt he would know who I was. He held a very senior rank, and as I said, in those days they were regarded as God.

CHAPTER SIX
FIRST POST TO WYTHALL

In 1979 Anne and I were still living at Loxley Close, and we had been there now for three years, and she had managed to get Paul into a local nursery. We had our tense moments, and for a short period, she moved back home to her parents. The stress of the job, at times, dictated my life. Having prisoners to be dealt with meant staying at work until the early hours, and that meant that Anne couldn't have much of a social life, so just around that time, it all got a bit too much. What didn't help was the type of people moving in around us. There was one family who had come from the Birmingham area, a couple with about seven kids, and the man was rough as dogs. He soon got to know I was a Police Officer and would make pig grunting noises as he passed the house. He owned a pit bull dog that roamed the street, and very often it would sit on the step of our front door, growling. It got to the stage where we were afraid to leave the house. If the dog was sitting there, I would throw a bowl of steaming hot water at it from an upstairs window to get it shifted away from our step.

Anne's living back at her parents was short-lived, and she came back when I promised to try and get us away from Loxley Close. I wanted to get out of Redditch full stop, but there were no Police houses, except one at 399 Alcester Road, Wythall, which was some 10 miles in the direction of Birmingham. The house was a large semi-detached property overlooking fields, with a large back garden. Wythall was a community with its own Police Station a few doors up from the two Police houses. The Police Station itself was a large building, made up of two offices with a house either side of the offices. There was direct access into the offices by either house, there was a garden to the one house and a parking area behind the other, as well as a frontage at the Station.

I loved my stint at Wythall - it was a really proactive posting, where I was left alone to hunt West Midlands villains. The West Midlands border was a couple of miles away, and it was a different type of Policing, with a lot less of the pressure of bigger towns. The Station worked on a twenty four-hour basis, with two

Sergeants and two Constables per shift, covering the twenty four- hour Policing, and there was also a small section Station at the village of Alvechurch, with a beat Constable, and one at Hopwood up the road from Alvechurch, and their mother Station was Wythall. Wythall patch was mainly rural and covered everything north of Redditch, taking in the Main A435 and A441 roads into Birmingham. The border was with West Midlands Police area at Maypole across to Kings Norton.

Wythall crime stemmed mainly from criminals crossing the border onto West Mercia.

Wythall village itself was mainly middle class, there was a small council estate and we also had a couple of pubs, as well as an established travellers' site on Hounsfield Lane.

It was no secret that around this time I was stale, getting very despondent, and that I needed to get away from Redditch. I often used to drop the hints to my shift Inspector that I wanted out. I put in a report, citing the domestic problems, highlighting the family around where I lived, and the fact that I owed it to my family to move away from Loxley Close. The house

399 Alcester Road was empty, and I was told that the property was for Sergeants, but that I would be allocated the house if I moved at my own expense.

The condition was, however, that if a Sergeant required it, I would have to move out.

In 1979 we moved, when Paul was three years old, or coming up to that age. The house was large and old, had single-glazed, galvanised windows, there was no central heating, and only storage heaters, which were useless. We were granted a decoration allowance, and the Force arranged for the place to be decorated within a certain budget. To Anne and me it was like a palace, and it lifted our spirits no end. Paul had been at a nursery on the Church Hill estate in Redditch on a part time basis, so had to give that up. We'd only been in our new home a week or so when there was a knock on the door. It was a woman who worked at the nursery and knew we had moved up to Wythall. She told Anne about a woman called Angela, who owned and ran a private preparatory school called Innisfree House on Station Road, Wythall. She was a friend of Angela's and had told her about Anne. The staff member from the nursery came to our house out of the blue and informed Anne that a job was going at Innisfree House School. Anne met Angela and she was offered a place, which she accepted, and she started working there full-time, and remained for many years. Paul was given a free place until he started state school at Meadow Green School in Wythall, so things were looking up.

By now I had a family car. We had managed to afford a couple of old bangers while at Redditch, and shortly after moving to 399 Alcester Road, I was posted to Wythall as well, so the only distance I had to travel to work was next door but one. One old banger I bought was probably the worst car I had ever owned. It was an old Morris Oxford, and it had an automatic gear box, the likes of which were quite rare in those days. It was probably manufactured fifteen years or so before we got it. It was blue, with a fair bit of rust, it had carpet, and rubber mats over the carpet, and it was cheap. I think I paid about £100, but it was all we could afford. We were still at Loxley Close when I bought it.

Within weeks the reverse gear packed up, so I was only able to go forwards, and had to make sure I didn't go anywhere where I needed to reverse. On the part of Loxley Close where I lived, the road was on a downhill slope, so each time I got home I had to turn in the junction so I could freewheel backwards down the slope. I had priced up a new gear box, but because they were rare it would have been way too expensive. In the end, I had to pay £80 for a mechanic to strip the box and replace some part or other that gave me back my reverse gear. He said it was a temporary repair.

What prompted me to do this was the day Anne and I went to a wedding. It was the wedding of Peter and Lynn, two shift members (Peter went on to become the Assistant Chief Constable). The wedding was in Worcester at a venue off the ring road, and I missed the entrance and stopped just after it. I didn't know the area and there were no satnavs then, so Anne had to get out in her best clothes and, placing her hands on the bonnet, to push the car back, with me half in and half out of the door, trying to assist with my right foot. After that I thought I'd better get this repaired. Later, water started to seep in under the carpet in the passenger footwell. I lifted the carpet and saw a gaping hole, and found that I was looking at the road surface. A quick trip Halfords was called for. I bought some fibreglass sheets and filler, sprayed it and replaced the carpet. Then I sold it on for £50.00.

It was a big relief to get away from Redditch, and I remained working at Wythall from 1980 until January 1985. Because of a leg injury I'd managed to pick up, I had to move back to Redditch, but remained living at 399 Alcester Road. Starting work at Wythall was so different from Redditch, because for one thing, we were not supervised twenty four hours a day, there were only two Sergeants, Geoff who lived in the house on the left of the Police station, and Dick. who lived in his own house in the village. We covered a large area, which was good, and we often hung around the border with West Midlands Police at Maypole and Kings Norton, as very often this was where it all kicked off.

We were controlled from Redditch, but the UHF radio system, being channel 32 at the time, was too far away, and we had to rely on the VHS car radio system. Our call sign was BM 32 on VHS and BA 32 on UHF. Ironically, Kings Heath Police Station, about four or five miles over the border, also operated on Channel

32, but the distance between Redditch and Kings Heath (about thirteen miles) was such that they never interfered with each other. We were able to speak to Kings Heath, whose call sign was Bravo 3 Control, even though the station was about 3 miles from Wythall station.

As a rule, we didn't call Kings Heath unless it was an extreme emergency; after all, they were West Midlands Police and not responsible for our patch. We would call and offer our assistance if there was a border incident, we would listen to their transmissions to hear what was going on, or make note of any suspicious activity involving cars in their area that might spill over onto ours.

One night, my partner and I were sitting in the office at Wythall, having our break. It was about two o'clock in the morning, and we heard the Kings Heath Controller call one of his patrols. It went something like this:

"Bravo 3 Control to Mike 1. Over."

"Go ahead, B3."

"Make your way to Maypole Island. There are sheep on the road."

"Will do, what do you suggest I do with them?"

"Chase them down the Alcester road onto West Mercia, then come away." I thought, you cheeky sod and I got onto the radio and said, "No, you don't, we are listening, you know."

B3 piped up over the airwaves after a brief silence,

"Mike 1, forget the West Mercia idea then, route them along Maypole Lane onto L1." (L1 was the Solihull Section of West Midlands Police.) And I assume this is what they did.

We were called out one night to a drunk on Hollywood lane. We moved him on, but he kept coming back, making a nuisance of himself, sitting on the roadside, singing.

He wasn't aggressive, just happy, and being a bloody pain in the arse. We kept getting calls about him, and the Sergeant at Redditch wouldn't be happy if we took him in there. So we put him into the Police car, and drove him to the Stratford Road at Shirley in West Midlands Police area, and dropped him off there, where he sat down and started singing again. Then we hotfooted it back to our own patch, leaving him to it. (Summary justice for the incident with the sheep?)

In every Police car, there is a mileage book, and each shift had to record the start and end mileage on their shift. Each month the sheet had to go to admin so they could monitor mileage and fuel costs.

At some point during my time at Wythall, I was working with Nick. He was a single man, who had originated in Rhodesia, as it was then. He sported a beard and spoke with a posh accent, but in reality, he was anything but posh. He was a nice and decent bloke. Nick and I worked together for some time, and became friends. After a time, he met a local woman a little older than him and had a relationship with her. Nick went to live in another Police House further into the village, and he got a small dog as well. Sometimes when we started in the mornings, we followed the nightshift of a couple of officers called Dave and Dave.

Now, Wythall could be very quiet during the night, particularly in the week, and you could go ages without getting any calls or seeing anyone about. So, you could either drive around all night, accumulating a lot of miles, or do what the two Daves often did, and spend it playing bar billiards at the Peacock Pub about three miles from the Station in the middle of nowhere. The Peacock was owned by a Welshman and his wife, and was a well- known tea stop at any time for all the Officers. They were rumbled when we used to check the mileage book and see only about ten miles recorded for a night shift, whereas we would clock up anything up to a hundred. They were not constantly in there, but it was a tea stop, and it seemed they were in there a lot, when they would have you believe they were out foot patrolling. Yeah, right, of course they were. The two Daves moved on to other parts of the Force, and I am not sure what became of them.

There was an eccentric character on the patch, who everyone got to know and dread dealing with. Her name was Beryl, an elderly woman who lived in a large mansion-type property on Druids Lane. Beryl was a problem for West Mercia, because her address fell in our remit. She was forever on the phone, making complaints about this and that, making all sorts of accusations against Officers. She was, by all accounts, not allowed to control her own finances and was a ward of court or something similar. I am talking over thirty years ago, and she had no family to speak of. I think she is probably long dead now, and I know the property was demolished years ago.

It is likely she had mental health issues, was allowed to live on her own, but not have control of decision making. Any Officer who went to her home was advised to go with a partner, because she was unpredictable, and she saw herself as upper class, whereas we were lower class. She would at times be ridiculed by the local Druids Heath miscreants, but West Midlands would always refer her to us.

I remember one day we were in the office and we saw her car pull onto the front of the Police station. I seem to recall there were about three or four of us in the station at the time. We all dived onto the floor, one of us quickly crawled to the front door and locked it, and we kept our heads down as she continued to ring the bell. (We often had to lock the station when we were out, but there was a phone at the front for the public that went through to HQ). We could hear her on the phone to some unfortunate person in the Force control room on the other end. She was moaning about the Police Station being closed, and was complaining about aliens of some sort invading her home. Complaints of this sort were common. An eccentric person who had some mental health problems, I suppose today she would be subject to some care in the community, but back then there was nothing, and like a lot of other things, this kind of provision is a change for the better.

It was during this period I attended my first murder scene. The body of a black woman was discovered one morning at Alderhanger Lane, a large lay-by hidden behind trees off the Main A435 dual carriageway. The lay-by used to attract lorry drivers, who parked up there overnight, and courting couples. It was right on the border with Warwickshire Police area, and when we arrived, a Warwickshire crew were already there. I was with the Sergeant, a man called Colin (I think), who was working at Wythall at the time, and who had replaced Dick or Geoff.

The body was just along the side road,

which was a lane with ditches either side. I didn't see the body, because the area had already been taped and cordoned off. Warwickshire had called out their senior Officers, and then it was decided that the body lay on West Mercia area, so West Mercia also called out senior Officers. There was a conference then between visiting senior Officers from both Forces, while the minions like me were watching from afar. They decided that West Mercia would take on the job, so Warwickshire went off. I was ordered to go back to Wythall to open up the Station, and be prepared for an influx of personnel, as it was likely a murder incident room would be set up there. I had to go and buy more milk and other essential supplies, while the circus continued at Alderhanger Lane. The body turned out to be a prostitute named Valerie Brown, an afro-Caribbean woman from the Handsworth area of Birmingham.

She had been murdered and her body dumped in the lay-by.

Over the course of the investigation, we had to make enquiries in the Lozells and Handsworth areas of Birmingham. One of the jobs was to distribute posters in local pubs, cafes and restaurants. This was my job, and I was given a load of posters and leaflets, headlined MURDER, with a photo of the victim and telephone numbers of the incident room.

Now, I hadn't been to the area of Handsworth or Lozells much, only a couple of times. It had a reputation as being the drug and crime capital of Birmingham, and it was well known for its ethnic population of black and Asian residents. This was a culture I had never really experienced and I didn't really know what to expect. (I had always lived a sheltered life.) I arranged my visit, or it might have been done for me, to report to Thornhill Road Police Station at Handsworth, where I was going to team up with a local Officer, (which gave me the confidence to go) and walk the streets of Lozells and Handsworth, visiting the cafes, clubs, pubs and other outlets, distributing the posters and leaflets. I went, not knowing what to expect, my fears were not realised, and I found the experience was good, rather than bad. I was dressed in my West Mercia uniform, the helmet slightly different from the one the Officer I was with was wearing. Locals picked up on this and a good many of them asked where I was from.

There had been no diversity training in those days, but that would all change later on with the fall-out over the murder of Stephen Lawrence, when it was suggested that the Metropolitan Police Force was institutionally racist. This report sent reverberations across the entire UK Police Service. Some may say that the diversity training that did come into play was a little over the top. I certainly remember there were some heated discussions in the training room, and some would not speak at all. I remember one senior Detective Inspector complaining to the trainer that he objected to being forced onto the training programme, and he took umbrage, because his interpretation of this coersion was that the management assumed we were all racists. It got to the stage where the trainer spoke to the class and no one would interact, for fear of saying the wrong thing. Everyone was paranoid that anything they said which was in disagreement with the management, would be noted and affect their careers.

While I was in Handsworth, I was taken to visit pubs where the landlords were mainly black, barbershops which were a mixture of black and Asian people, and dubious-looking clubs, where lots of young men were hanging out, a completely different set up from what I was used to. Some people had long dreadlocks and wore brightly-coloured woollen hats. A truly diverse area, and I found the officer I was with was known in most of the places we visited. We gave out the posters and asked people to display them. The investigating Officers believed that the victim was murdered elsewhere, and her body driven to Alderhanger lane.

Eventually an arrest was made and a man convicted of her murder. It was quite a good feeling, in a funny sort of way, to be involved in my first murder. I say involved, if attending the scene, and then arranging the tea pot back at the Station, can be called involvement. I suppose attending the Lozells area was playing a part, albeit a small one.

CHAPTER SEVEN
THE MINERS STRIKE BACK

On 1st April 1983 Anne and I moved into our first bought house. We were determined not to move back to Redditch. We bought a small semi-detached house in a cul-de-sac in the Wythall area. I first had to apply, via a written report, for permission to buy my own house and for the location to be approved. House prices were quite high in the Wythall area, compared to the new town at Redditch. Even with Anne's salary and mine put together, we could not afford much. I discovered the house we were to buy at one o'clock one morning in late 1982. I'd been called by the next door neighbour, who told me that a domestic dispute was taking place next door. I got there to find the woman living at the address, and the owner, in tears. There was an acrimonious divorce going on and a court order was in place to sell the house and split the proceeds between the warring couple. I told Anne the next morning and once I'd persuaded her that this house was affordable, we started the process, and we eventually bought the house for £23,500.

We had a 100% mortgage. The house

was in a poor state, it needed central heating, as it had none, and the windows were tatty. The woman living there had a large sheepdog that lived in the lounge, and the house stank and was filthy. The back garden consisted of an overgrown lawn and weeds. The carpet in the dining/kitchen area was matted, and had been nailed down in various places to hold it in place. The wooden single glazed windows were rotting in places too. We saw the potential, and we planned to stay there a couple of years before moving up the property ladder. Thirty four years later and we are still there, although it looks much different now, having had extensions built and other alterations made. Anne's Dad went nuts when he saw it, but we knew it had potential. It was our first home.

In 1984 Margaret Thatcher was Prime Minister. Some said she was a formidable woman who was intent on taking on the Trade Unions. Part of the car giant British Leyland complex fell within West Mercia, and there was a very well-known Trade Unionist there known as Red Robbo. His correct name was Derek Robinson, and he seemed to be at the centre of strikes at the plant, and was always on the news holding forth about the government of the day, and workers' rights. In those days, there were a lot of strikes by various trades and professions, and it was a case of the unions having, or appearing to have, the capability of holding the country to ransom. Margaret Thatcher was a determined woman, and she took on the Unions and introduced legislation to curb their militant ways. Of course, there were always those who would not take this lying down, and battlelines were drawn with the more militant unions.

One such union was the National Union of Mineworkers. In the 1970s the miners were in dispute with the Prime Minister Ted Heath's Conservative Government. The country was nearly brought to its knees; there were power cuts daily, TV channels shut down at ten o'clock in the evening, and workers were on a three-day week, as coal was in short supply to fuel the power stations. The Yorkshire miners descended on Saltley coke works in Birmingham, and staged a mass picket, causing the place to shut down.

Birmingham City Police were overwhelmed that day and in the interests of safety, had to shut the place down. Arthur Scargill, who led the Yorkshire miners that day, saw this as a great victory for Union Power. He was one of the most militant union leaders of that day. Arthur Scargill was said by some to be a left-wing activist and anti-establishment. The actions of the miners at Saltley brought down the Conservative Government and the Prime Minister, Edward Heath. When Margaret Thatcher came to power in 1979, she was determined to take on the might of the militant unions. The new Conservative Government, headed by Margaret Thatcher, had appointed an American business man, Ian Macgregor, as the head of the National Coal Board. He had formerly worked for British Leyland and British Steel, both nationalised companies that have since been sold off.

Margaret Thatcher was hailed as a great leader by some, and loathed by others. I drink on a Wednesday night with a group of friends, and one of them, a man who works in the private sector, loathed her, and blames her for many of the country's ills today. He blames her for the closure of the car industry, the steel industry and the coal mines. Whenever her name pops up in our weekly discussions he gets his hackles up. I find it quite amusing to wind him up. If the conversation ever flags on a Wednesday evening I only have to mention her name, and suggest what a great leader she was, and he will get on his soap box. He always told us he had a bottle of champagne in the fridge waiting to be opened the day she passed on. Indeed, when that day arrived, 8th April 2013, he phoned us all up to say he had cracked the bottle open. Today's topic to get him all wound up is Brexit, because he is a staunch remoaner. But hey, that's a story for another time.

But I digress. Back to Ian Macgregor. His job was to get the mining industry to pay its way, and the Unions opposed him and the Government, because it inevitably meant that many mines would have to shut down. This resulted in the conflict with the National Union of Mineworkers calling for an all-out strike.

The Police Service played a major role throughout this dispute, something that the Service had never experienced before or since. Fourty three Police Forces of England and Wales would, within a few weeks of the start of the miners' strike, become organised. Their central point was the main command centre for the organising of mutual aid. This came in the form of Police Support Units to the Police Forces affected by this influx of mass pickets. Wherever there was a mining community, the Force in that area was affected. West Yorkshire, and South Yorkshire, Arthur Scargill's territory, had the most mines and mining communities.

These communities were very loyal to Arthur Scargill, or King Arthur, as he was known. They relied on the mines for their living, and there were many families whose elders and ancestors had worked in the mines. Other areas included Warwickshire, Staffordshire and Nottinghamshire. These areas were not as militant, and some of the miners wanted to carry on working. There was a large steelworks in Scunthorpe that relied on coal to carry on production, as well as power stations across the country, and all of these were potentially the subject of mass picketing by the NUM.

It was not known at the time, but the government had been stockpiling coal at the power stations for some time. This betrayed the turn of events that the government expected. The secret stockpiling of coal at the power stations had wrongfooted Scargill. The strike lasted for over twelve months, throughout 1984 until the early part of 1985, when the miners realised that they were not going to achieve their objectives. The role of the Police was mainly to keep the peace, and to assure the safety of those wishing to work, as it was their right to do. Even in the main heartlands of the Yorkshire pits, some miners wanted to work, and this caused many a feud, and intimidation, which, for some people still exists to this day.

Now, I only ever spent five or six weeks away from home, but other Officers were away a lot longer. We were well paid, the Home Office picking up the bill. For the likes of Officers from West Mercia, we were mainly sent on rest days. At the time, I was working as a Constable at Wythall, and there were only two Officers per shift, so we at Wythall did not get to be that involved. The Duties Officer at Divisional HQ at Redditch had the task of selecting which Officers would be sent on the PSUs. As I said, it was lucrative for those who were sent. Officers from specialist departments such as CID and Traffic were not really involved, as the majority of them were not trained in public order tactics. Those left behind were often working twelve-hour shifts to cover for those who were away. Only one Officer at Wythall went away on the PSU per week, if at all. Any of the Police Forces wanting mutual aid had to put their request to the Central Command in London, which had been set up for the dispute. Each force would be contacted to arrange mutual aid. West Mercia normally sent one full PSU from each Division.

A PSU would consist of one Inspector, two Sergeants and twenty Constables. So each PSU had the use of two personnel vehicles, each capable of carrying twelve persons, and a transit van for carrying the kit, such as suit cases, riot shields and PSU clothing. There were seven Divisions in West Mercia at that time, so that would be twenty one vehicles, some of which had to be hired, particularly the vans for the kit. Most weeks, West Mercia would send PSUs, mainly up north. On the occasions that I went, we were billeted at the REME barracks at Kirton Lindsey, about five miles from Scunthorpe. Our role was mainly connected with the large steelworks at Scunthorpe, but one or two of our PSUs would travel into either

West Yorkshire or South Yorkshire, if required, to be on standby. West Mercia Force, like others, would assemble on a Sunday and travel in a convoy to their appointed destination, the front and rear vehicles with their blue lights on.

It was quite a sight, I can tell you, seeing a long line of moving Police vans travelling along the motorways and side roads, and the ironic thing is that we would pass, or see, other convoys of Police vans from other Forces travelling to their appointed places. The Service had never seen anything like it. It took a few weeks for the logistics and organisation to be properly coordinated, and when it was, it worked well. There had been a lot in the news in the run-up to the strike, and negotiations had broken down. There was no ballot, as I recall, in those days, and Scargill ordered an all-out strike. I first got involved at the start. I was on a two-ten shift and it was afternoon time when I had a call to go, as Warwickshire Police had requested assistance to a possible mass picket at collieries at Coventry and Daw Mill. I was told to bring an overnight bag with me. It was all very rushed and within a couple of hours, other Officers had been called in, and like me, some were on two-ten shift. We assembled at Redditch and were briefed that the strike had started, that there was picketing, and intelligence suggested that mass pickets were arriving at the collieries. Warwickshire Police, being a small Force, needed assistance. We were told we might be on until the morning before we'd be able to come back. We assembled the PSU and drove to a military barracks at Sutton Coldfield. We were fed, and then out we went and parked up somewhere in the countryside to await further orders. Nothing happened that night, but unbeknown to us at the time, arrangements were being made for this to be a weeklong occurrence, and we arrived back at the barracks the next morning, where we were told that we would be staying the rest of the week.

Army makeshift cot beds were up and sleeping bags, and we were told to get some kip and be ready at six o'clock that evening. We were given meal times. The force was also arranging for our families to send clothing and toiletries for the week. My in-laws lived not very far away, so they arranged, via Anne, to bring a suitcase to me, with clothing and toiletries. The sleeping arrangements were not desirable. "Hot-bedding" was the order of the day. That's where one person moved into a bed just vacated by another. Other Forces had supplied Officers, and for this first week we had to sleep using sleeping bags provided by the military. The trouble was that they were shared, so when we got back at six o'clock in the morning, we climbed into a bag which had just been slept in by someone else.

It was this week at the start of the strike that I saw some action. I didn't get involved in any other action from then on, despite going away a further five times throughout that year. In those days, I had done public order and shield training. But the intensity of the training today has changed dramatically from those days. Our role was to prevent a breach of the peace and uphold the law and people's right to work. This incident happened late in the afternoon one day. The place was Kersley colliery at Coventry on the road outside the main gates to the Colliery. A large crowd of people, mainly men, had assembled. I'm not sure where they had come from, but there were about a hundred and fifty of them, shouting and chanting, and it was all very jovial, and not causing a problem. They were there to prevent any coal lorries entering or leaving the site.

Our PSU was lined up along the street, when suddenly the crowd surged and blocked the road and the entrance to the gates. Part of our training in crowd control was something called a "wedge". A wedge was a number of officers that would link arms and stand at an angle, and basically, we were shaped as a group into a wedge with one person at the front and those behind expanding outwards. Now, with me being one of the smaller officers, on the command from the Inspector to "Form a wedge!" I was positioned about third from the front man. I had only ever been in a wedge during training up until then.

The idea of a wedge was to trudge forwards with a side-stepping movement into a crowd and the idea was that the crowd would be forced to split, a bit like Moses parting the Red Sea. It worked in training, where we parted about twenty Police cadets, but we'd never tried it where the crowd was about a hundred or so. Again, I'm reliably informed that this tactic is still in use today. Hell, if was good enough for the Romans…

We formed our wedge, and the

Inspector, who, by the way, was at the back, ordered us to trudge forwards. This was the first time I'd been in this type of operation, where there was the potential for a large confrontation. The training kicked in, but I admit I was nervous, if not a little apprehensive. We slowly entered the mass and the sheer weight of the Officers in the wedge forced part of the crowd to split, and so then we were side-stepping into the crowd. The pressure of the weight of the line to my right was becoming so intense that the sides of my torso were being squeezed. So much that I was lifted off the ground, and carried along with the rest of the wedge. I was the smallest, and I was trapped, there was nothing I could do. I was hoping the pressure on me wouldn't intensify, because I was getting scared my rib cage might get damaged. The wedge worked, the crowd split and we achieved our goal. I am glad I never had to go through that again throughout my service.

There were no arrests and at the end of that first week we went home and were given a couple of days off, and they paid us for sixteen-hour shifts for that week. My next time away was a few weeks later. All the organisation on the part of the Police for handling the strike was in place by then. Likewise, the miners themselves were organised and coordinated, and they had a system for mobilising their pickets. It was a game of cat and mouse, where the Police did not let on where they would be, and the miners did not let on what their intentions were. As far as possible, the Police had to be ready to react at short notice, and put in place PSUs at strategic points.

For the most part, as mentioned, West Mercia was used mainly for the steelworks. During the five separate weeks I attended, I saw no action, and the long sixteen-hour shifts were at times quite boring. We travelled up on a Sunday, arriving late in the afternoon. The dormitories consisted of bunk beds, a small locker and a number of men in one place. There was no privacy, and the washrooms and showers were in a block nearby. I wasn't used to living like this, but I was part of a disciplined service and I had to knuckle down like the rest of them. There were a lot of different personalities, there were some who even relished being away and treated it like some sort of holiday.

Despite working from three in the morning and not getting back to camp until seven o'clock at night, some Officers would get changed and hit the nearby town, and be back an hour or so before we hit the road again at three o'clock the next morning. Those same Officers caught up on their sleep in the back of the van during the day. The kit van allowed for two sleepers, providing the shields were laid in such a way to act as a bed base. One particular character that was on the PSU was a short chap, with blond hair, albeit thinning on top, known as Sticky, although his proper name was Nigel. Nigel was one of those likable characters, who everyone got on with. He had an infectious personality, and what baffled all his male colleagues at the time was his ability to pull women. He was a babe magnet, and for the life of me I really don't know why. My wife always used to say, "Ah, he's lovely, he's cute." (Sick-bucket, quick, someone please.) He was suave and smooth, a somewhat cheeky chap, who liked to play the odd practical joke. Always had a smile on his face and nothing ever appeared to faze him.

One evening we arrived back at the barracks after a long day, and Nigel went out and arrived back on a pedal cycle about thirty minutes before we hit the road. Story has it he had met a girl, went back to her place and used her pedal cycle to get back to the camp on time. He rode up to the gates, so he said, and flashed a card, shouting "kitchen staff" at the guard, and rode straight in. He handcuffed the cycle to the bed frame of his bunk bed. While he was away, someone had removed the saddle and wheels, and all that was left there was a frame. This was one of many things that took place to keep our spirits up. At the end of the week the PSU that Nigel was attached to put the pedal cycle into the kit van, and then the three vans drove to where the girl lived and gave the cycle back. That must have been a sight for the neighbours. seeing a full PSU contingent outside their houses to return a cycle.

There was a TV room with a video player at the barracks for our use. It was a waste of time going in there to catch up on the soaps or news, as more often than not, they were watching serious porn, and the room was packed full of lecherous men, some of whom had to resort to standing on chairs to peer through the skylight above the entrance door.

There were card schools taking place, where money was changing hands. There was one lad, Alex. Alex was well known for being a bit gullible, a likable chap, he would never make it past the rank of Constable. People took the mickey out of him all the time, and he was often the butt of practical jokes. In today's world, I would go as far as to say he was being bullied. He liked to play poker, and the others used to encourage him to up his stakes. One evening it got out of hand, where serious money was changing hands, and an Inspector got to hear about it, and he put a stop to it. The days were long, we would get out of bed at two in the morning, have a greasy breakfast in the Naffi, and pile into our personnel carriers and be on the road at three. Although we were there for the steelworks, I never actually got to the place, and I don't think any of my co-officers there did either.

We were there doing a job, ready to react to any pickets arriving at the steelworks. It wasn't just West Mercia, every Police Force in the land had a contingent of PSUs somewhere in the UK, where there were coalmines or industries reliant on coal. The miners were out to shut these places down, to bring the government down. On a personal note, I felt I was doing my duty for Queen and country. I was opposed to militant unions, and particularly to the likes of Scargill, and Red Robbo, the militant unionist at the Longbridge car plants, who was lambasted by the press back in the seventies for the problems at the plant. On my first day working on the footplate section, in the training room at British Rail, ASLEF train drivers' Union had me join ASLEF. It was a closed shop, which meant if I refused to join, I had no job, and so I had no choice. The unions saw Thatcher as a threat, and imagined that she was using the Police Forces as her personal army, and as a means to achieve her goal.

The days were long, mainly spent sitting for two hours on a bridge over a motorway somewhere near Scunthorpe, in the Humber region. We would do about two hours at a time, and then be relieved by another unit.

We would then go off to a small cricket club somewhere, and stay there for two hours, before starting the cycle again.

Before leaving the barracks, each van was given a bin liner which had wrapped-up sandwiches for the day, with crisps, apples and a selection of soft drinks and water. In those days, there was no concern about food poisoning, no keeping the food cool, and during the summer it was not unusual to be scoffing warm ham sandwiches and drinking luke-warm pop. We would get a hot meal during the day, at a pre-arranged diner or some other venue. Roast chicken dinner at nine in the morning was not unusual. Our time was basically on standby, in case the pickets decided to target the steelworks, or block roads to prevent the convoy of coal lorries keeping the steelworks going. Boredom was a factor, sitting around so much. Those who had not bothered going to bed would sleep, others would sit at makeshift tables at the side of the van, playing cards, or just reading papers. Occasionally there would be banter, and I remember one particularly childish prank that, yet again, Alex was the focus of. Alex was sitting in the back of the van, reading a newspaper, and someone thought it would be funny to light the corner of his paper with a naked flame. Alex didn't see the funny side and refused to put it out, laying it on the floor, while everyone piled out of the van. It took someone sensible to stamp out the flames. I was one of the ones to make a fast exit.

Throughout 1984, as I said, I went to Kirton Lindsey five times. With the extra money I earned in overtime, I managed to buy a second-hand Vauxhall car. While I was away during the summer, Anne and our son Paul contracted chicken pox, but luckily for me, I was not there to get infected. The strike eventually ended in the early part of 1985, and the miners went back to work, resigned to the fact they were not going to win. Relationships between the miners and the Police from that day were strained, and the Forces who Policed those areas had some extensive bridge building to do.

Outside Sheffield was the British Steel Coking plant at Orgreave, and this was a major event, if not the most significant event to have taken place during the strike. I wasn't there, but like the rest of the country, I witnessed what was taking place on the television news. It was the 18th June 1984, and some five thousand miners had descended on the plant, intent on blockading the place to prevent the movement of coal, a repeat of the Saltley event in Birmingham. It was an operation the Police absolutely had to win to gain overall control. There was a heavy Police contingent which included Police horses, from Forces all over the country. The operation in Police terms went as well as could be expected, there was violence on both sides, and we all saw images of Police horses charging into the crowd, and miners being whacked around the head by truncheon-wielding officers. Likewise, there were images of miners kicking and assaulting Officers. I was glad I was not there; it must have been frightening for all involved. There has been a lot of criticism about the Police tactics on that day, as well as of individual Officers.

It must be remembered that Police Officers are human, and when faced with such a hostile crowd, remembering at that time this was unprecedented, adrenalin would be running very high, and those individual Officers lashing out were probably in a state of defensiveness. Coppers are humans, and all humans have the fight or flight mechanism. The difference is that the Officers had to be more fight than flight, they were there under a disciplined regime, and they were trained to stand their ground. The miners, on the other hand, were by large an undisciplined crowd. They believed their way of life was under threat, they saw the Police as an arm of the oppressors, and they did not focus on the individual person behind the Uniform. The press had also hyped up this day, and the recipe for a day of violence was laid bare for all to see.

Scargill got himself arrested, the TV cameras filming him, and he played to the watching press and cameras, making some half-hearted effort to tell the audience he hadn't done anything, but this was all part of his publicity strategy. The tactics used by the Police were designed to make sure they had the upper hand. They had to win the day for the sake of the country, but doubtless there will be those who would disagree.

This event is still talked about some thirty three years later, with some calling for a public enquiry into the Police actions, along with allegations of corruption and cover-up. It remains to be seen if anything further comes of this after this length of time. There were many stories told about those days, of the behaviour of some Officers, which I can well believe to be true. Stories such as Officers goading miners on the picket line about the amount of money they were earning, flashing five pound notes at them, and generally winding them up. I did not witness this myself, but the papers were reporting it, and the Metropolitan Police were singled out in particular for the insensitivity of some of their Officers.

The strike also attracted other stories about the indiscretions of individual Officers, one being from West Mercia. One Officer from the Force not known to me personally, appeared one day on the front pages of the tabloids, the story alleging he was playing away from home with a woman, or women. I don't know whether this was a true story or not. My days on the miners' strike ended in the first week of January 1985. I was due to go away in the second week on annual leave, and unfortunately, I broke my ankle while playing with my son on holiday.

It also ended my time at Wythall in the rank of Constable, (only to return years later as a Sergeant) and I had to go back to Redditch on light duties.

As with most things in life, things happen and then they come to an end. Margaret Thatcher was no exception; she was to some a good Prime Minister, but not to all; a Marmite sort of person.

The Falklands War was another legacy she is remembered for. That war was in 1982, when she was hailed as a great leader. Some likened her to Churchill, because she took no nonsense from the Argentines. She took them on, regained the Falklands and won the war. Her popularity had begun to wane about that time, and they say the Falklands conflict won her the next election, allowing her to take on the miners.

I wonder how things might have turned out if there had been no Falklands Conflict, and she never had never won that election. Perhaps the next Government, which was Labour, might have done things differently. After all, the Labour Party has to rely on the Unions to survive.

It's all "what ifs".

CHAPTER EIGHT
PRANKS AND PROMOTIONS

Having recovered fully from my broken ankle, I started back on full-time duties at Redditch, working twenty four hour shifts. The shift Inspector was a man named Tony. I had a difficult relationship with him, and I knew that for some reason he had taken a dislike to me. It seemed to me that he lacked any interest in me, and often said derogatory things to me.

As I mentioned near the start of this book, some people I got on with and some I did not. The Marmite syndrome. Tony was one of those that I did not. His attitude towards me caused me to lose confidence, and made me feel like staying at home. It was pointless complaining to the higher ranks, it was something you never did. I bided my time and tried to keep out of his way, knowing he would be retiring soon.

In my view, he looked upon me as someone who was never going to go beyond the rank of Constable, and he also gave me the impression that he was not enjoying his job, and was biding his time for retirement. He did eventually go, and I think he went after twenty five years' service. Some Officers had signed up for twenty five years, at the end of which their pension would kick in, and Tony was one of these.

I was now thirty one years old, I had been in the service for eleven years, had been married for ten years and had a nine-year-old son. I had to think about how my career was going. I was never an academic, and I knew I would not be destined for high ranks. I decided I would give the promotional Sergeant's Exam a go, because it would give me something to focus on. I began to study and I eventually passed the exam, which consisted of three papers. Passing this exam gave me a great sense of achievement. Others I knew who had taken the exam had failed, even though they were more academic than me.

The fact that I had no educational qualifications and had been in a low stream at school was always at the back of my mind, and played a part in my lack of confidence. It was all very well having passed the exam, but getting promoted was now the hard bit. It was up to me at that point to show that I had the acumen and the ability to become a Sergeant, to take on the extra responsibilities.

I knew in the back of my mind that I could do the job, but, more importantly, I had to prove myself to senior ranks. I was also getting a bit stale working the streets, patrolling and dealing with the day to day routine of domestics, and mundane jobs. In short, I was getting in a rut and needed a change. I fancied the idea of working in the Divisional control room as a Controller, the Officer who would grade incoming calls, dispatch the appropriate patrol and generally run any ongoing incident.

In those days, the control room consisted of a Controller, normally two civilian assistants, and a switchboard operator, although this last position was mainly a part-time post. There was also, at times, a Sergeant in there.

I knuckled down and worked hard. I seem to remember that the two Sergeants on the shift while I was still patrolling were Dave and Rod. I had some good arrests, and dealt with some protracted jobs. I won't go into the boring aspects of them but, needless to say, I took pride in my statement-taking, and report-writing.

I had a good yearly appraisal, and it was mentioned that I was looking for eventual promotion. By 1986 I was working in the control room as a Controller, and by now my supervisors were Inspector Chris, and the Sergeants were Pete and Brian.

The assistant controllers were Wendy One and Wendy Two, I mentioned these two at the start of this book. By now my confidence had picked up, and I was happy in the role. I received praise from the supervisors for my ability to manage the patrols on the street, make sure appropriate responses were made, and to manage those who attended. Police patrol Officers were inclined to converge on an incident and to run the risk of an over-the-top response. I always risk-assessed the job, and if I thought it needed a few more patrols, I made sure that those Officers were in place. In other words, I graded each job appropriately. I always nominated an Officer to attend, normally the Officer assigned to that beat. I was also mindful of other resources available, namely Traffic Officers and motorcyclists, who were not part of the Divisional resource, but who might be in the area. Traffic Officers worked out of HQ at Hindlip, and were controlled by HQ control room. These Officers were mostly supervised by other shift Controllers. Dog handlers were another resource I could call on, as well as the outlying beat Officers, from areas such as Alvechurch, and Inkberrow. I thoroughly enjoyed my role as a Controller. The best years of my career started from this point, and so did the banter and practical jokes.

The shift was made up of new recruits as well as some established Officers like myself. I was one of the senior Constables, having twelve years' service. My colleagues there included Alex, Clive, Jill, Mark, Jan (the same Jan who took to the athletics track) Glyn, who Jan would later marry, and Liz to name a few. There was also a girl named Isabell, who Alex used to have a soft spot for. It was around this time that my sense of humour kicked in. Call me childish if you like, but some of the pranks that we used to get up to as a shift were funny. These days, however, they would be frowned upon, and to some extent I suspect would probably not happen. Being a Controller Constable, you were expected to be making decisions on deployment, and the civilian operators would look to you for advice on what resources to deploy. Looking back, this role gave me a good grounding for moving up to the next rank.

The control room in those days was on the second floor, the public front office was on the ground floor, and the cell block was through a door on the ground floor adjacent to the front office. Very often, if there was nobody manning the front office during the night, members of the public would press a button, and we in the control room often had to run down the stairs. Eventually a CCTV camera was fitted into the front office, and a phone for the public to dial 0, and then we could speak to them from the control room. If necessary, I sent an Officer to the front office if they needed a face to face consultation. This would normally only happen in the early hours. Also in the front office was a public pay phone. We had many a giggle on nights when things were quiet. Of course, we knew the phone number to the public telephone. It was not unusual on a Friday night in the early hours of Saturday for the odd drunk to wander into the front office and use the seating.

From the control room, we used to ring the public phone and watch on the TV monitor in the control room for the reactions. Some would ignore the phone ringing. and others would answer. When someone answered, I would put on a voice and pretend to be a member of the public making a call to the Police station. I used to create character voices, which I used on several occasions. These pranks took place in the early hours, and I usually played them on unsuspecting young men who were the worse for wear, hanging around the front office. The two Wendys would be giggling in the back ground. Sometimes they would look at the CCTV and encourage me to phone down. We only made these calls to the public phone when there was only one person in the front office.

Sometimes a PC would be on duty in the front counter until two in the morning I used to pick my target and dial the number of the public phone, eagerly watching the monitor in the control room. I could see the target looking at the phone, then looking around. Remember, the phone in the public area is a pay phone for the use of the public. I let it ring and sometimes the target got up and had the courage to pick the receiver up, but first he would often peer into the front office through the screen, and only pick up the phone if he couldn't attract anyone's attention. Passing the handset through the opening in the security screen, the Officer would then realise it was me, and tell the stooge to leave it with him. Then he'd abuse me down the phone. I wasn't the only one to play this prank, by the way. It was childish, I know, it was not big and not clever. But it was funny, though.

Wendy Two was partial to the odd chocolate bar, and I often use to hide it in the freezer compartment in the control room fridge, much to her annoyance. She'd arrive at work at ten o'clock in the evening, and the first thing she would do was put her Mars Bar in the fridge to keep it cool. Then, when she wasn't looking, I'd put it in the small ice box. Four hours or so later she would go to eat it, and find it missing, and I'd be in the corner, giggling like a child. Then giggle even more as she tried to bite into a frozen Mars Bar. Wendy One, the older of the two, called me childish, but she laughed along as well. We all worked as a team, we got on well, and when things were busy and there was no time to pratt about, we knuckled down and made sure things were running smoothly and the job was getting done.

In later years, when we all moved on, and I am talking about twenty years or so later, Wendy Two had moved to HQ, Wendy One had left and moved to Cyprus, after her husband died suddenly. Anne and I met up with Wendy One in Cyprus, where she put us up at her place, and showed us the sights. Sadly, Wendy's life was cut short at a young age, when she became ill with some type of skin cancer, and she returned to the UK. She died while still in her fifties.

I wasn't the only one who took part in and arranged the odd prank. I remember one Sergeant, who has since passed on, had a habit of telling new recruits that they had to pass a cycling test. He said it was part of the training programme, in the way that they couldn't drive Police cars without first going on a driving course. Normally on a Sunday morning, cones were placed around the car park, and he would have them cycling in and out of the cones, while he ticked off an imaginary form on a clip board.

Or the raising of the flag on the flag pole on the Queen's birthday, and other special occasions when we'd have a recruit probationer standing in full uniform at seven o'clock in the morning, next to the pole, saluting and singing God Save The Queen. Other pranks which mainly occurred at night involved sending a probationer to the local cemetery, with other Officers hiding amongst the gravestones, making groaning noises. All very childish, but very funny at the time.

The keys to the Police vehicles were kept in a cabinet and there was always a spare set. One evening during a quiet moment, we thought it would be funny if someone were to find their Police car missing. You guessed it, we used the spare key to remove a parked Police car from the street, while the Officer using it was away, only to return to find it missing. We waited for his call to come in to say his Police car had been stolen, and then we questioned the Officer over the radio to make sure where he'd left it, that he'd locked it, and that he'd still got the keys on him. Then someone would call up to say they'd found it parked a street away from where he'd left it, and then we ribbed him that he'd forgotten where he'd parked it. This prank happened at other stations I worked at throughout the years.

I remember one example during my time

as a Controller, when one of the shift Sergeants was upset, because one of the Constables had been taking the piss out of him, just generally larking about. So he said he would have him during the night, and he asked me, at some point in the early hours, to send this particular Officer to a situation where he would have to get out of his Police car and walk quite a way from it. Meanwhile the Sergeant briefed the other shift members on the plan, and told them not to go and assist the Officer if he asked for it. They should say over the radio that they were committed, or make up some excuse. I can't recall all the details. I think I might have sent him to Arrow Valley Park to the screaming sound of a woman in distress. We very often got this type of call, which mainly turned out to be vixens having an old-fashioned equivalent of a tender meet-up with a lucky male fox. The job was set up, I called the Officer on the radio system, and the Sergeant was there, hidden away with the spare set of keys. He waited for the unfortunate Officer to arrive and park up, secure his car and, torch in hand, wander off into the darkness for a nice long walk into the parkland. Meanwhile the Sergeant, using the spare keys, simple drove the couple of miles or so back to the Police Station, parked up, and came into the Control room to wait for a radio call from the Constable, reporting his Police car missing. He didn't have to wait long. We all waited with anticipation to hear what he was likely to say.

Now I can picture the scene.

The Officer walking around the park, shining his torch here and there, probably thinking to himself, that Mr and Mrs Fox were having a good time in the open, and deciding there was nothing for the Police to see around there, and then moving on, making his way back to the car park. I imagined he walked to the car park, surprised to see his nice shiny Police car not there. And then he thought to himself,

"Did I park it here, or did I park it at the other car park just up the road?" No, he was certain he parked it there. He checked his pockets and pulled out his Police car key, and satisfied himself he hadn't left the keys in the car.

I imagined him getting a little worried and walking to the edge of the car park, where it joins the road, and him looking both ways.

No, it's not there.

He drew the conclusion that it had been nicked.

The call came in,

"Bravo-Alpha from two-three, I am in the park and I think someone's nicked my patrol car." The Sergeant took the radio handset, and with a big grin on his face spoke down the radio.

Sgt: "What do you mean, someone's nicked your Police car?"

PC: "Like I said, I parked it in the car park and now it's gone. Can you alert other patrols? It had my case and paperwork in there."

Sgt: "Did you leave it unlocked?"

PC: (whose voice is now sounding a little worried) "No, I still have the keys with me."

Sgt "Right, get yourself back here pronto and make out a report. All patrols, observations for PC Named vehicle. Appears to have been stolen from Arrow valley park area."

PC: "Bravo-Alpha, can someone come and pick me up please?"

Sgt: "No. They are out looking for the car you have lost, get back here as soon as, please, you will have to walk in."

The Officer walked back to the station, and as soon as he walked into the Station car park, there was his car, and the penny dropped. He stormed into the operations room, realising he had been duped, and the Sergeant told him never to take the piss out of him again. He took it in his stride, and this was just another example of pranks designed in some way to keep the shift tight and close. After all, you're happy if you have a happy team, and more work gets done.

In the centre of Redditch there is a number of multi-storey car parks, one of which we knew as car park two. This car park had strategically placed fire hoses on reels. Many an Officer had a good soaking from one of those during the night. Most of us on the receiving end of these pranks took it in the good spirit that it was intended, and it made for a happy team, and it cultivated the camaraderie we shared. I read about similar sorts of goings on in Forces all over the UK, and it's not just the Police. I should imagine it's the same for any tightly knit close working teams, such as the armed forces and fire service.

A good friend of mine, now retired, was in the West Midlands Police Force and he was a Controller for a short time at Kings Heath. He relayed a funny story to me. It was just after the Force helicopter was introduced, it was a warm evening, dark and quiet, and they set up a newbie, a probationer. They told the probationer that the Force helicopter was about to take off at Birmingham airport on some night training exercise. They were going to fly over the Kings Heath area, and they were training to spot movements at night, in particular, to identify Police Officers on the ground.

My friend Roger primed the probationer to go onto a flat part of the building's roof, have his radio with him and a torch, and once the helicopter was airborne they would call him up with instructions. Now, utilising an electric fan and a stiff piece of card to flicker against the spinning fan blades, in the radio room near the radio mike, Roger then called the probationer on the roof. He told me that he put on his best RAF pilot voice. He said, with the stiff card running along the fans blade, that he hoped the probationer would hear it and believe it was the sound of rotor blades in the back-ground. Roger was pretending to be an Officer on the helicopter, and was asking the probationer to switch on his torch and wave it frantically in the air so they could spot him. I must admit I thought about using that one myself.

Each Sub-Division in those days had its own control rooms, and controlled its own towns. Headquarters had a much larger control room that oversaw the entire Force, and should there be a major incident they would be the king pin, and they would take control. There was a Force Duty Control Room Inspector who would be calling the shots. That never happened to me while I worked in the local Redditch control room. The good thing about local Sub-Divisional control was that you had good local knowledge of your area, Redditch and Wythall being the area we patrolled. You got to know the crime hotspots, the local villains, the nooks and crannies of the entire patch, and the footpaths and side roads where criminals were likely to run and hide. I could direct Officers to strategic points around the area to cut off any escape routes offenders might have taken, were or likely to take. The new, centralised control room at Headquarters meant the demise of the local control room, and with it, the loss of,all this local knowledge.

There is in existence a DVD of a life in the day of a Controller, or rather an afternoon of a Controller. It was one summer's afternoon in 1986 or thereabouts. Nigel, or "Sticky", was performing the role of drugs liaison officer on the Division. Nigel owned a video recorder. Not the type you see today which, of course, are incorporated into mobile phones. This recorder was large, and the actual camera had a long cable leading to a box that contained the video cassette, and the box hung around your shoulder via a strap. Some of Anne's relatives had been over for a family barbecue and Nigel loaned me the video so we could record the event, and send a copy to relatives in Australia. I went back to work on the Monday on a two till ten shift, intending to return the device to Nigel. He just happened to be off that day, so I thought it a good idea to record around the station. It was a time when a young recruit had just started on the Shift. His name was Mark; he is the first to appear on the video. The video lasts about thirty minutes, and stars on the day included Sergeant Pete, Inspector Chris, Jill, Mark, Liz, Alex, Gary, and Godfrey, plus others who just happened to be coming my way on that day. I learned recently that a lot of people have somehow got copies of this, and watching it today shows how things have changed. I once showed the DVD to a rather straight-laced Inspector. I showed it to her again about ten years further on, and she told me to get rid of it, as it was not entirely politically correct; certainly, by today's standards it isn't. I know she found it amusing, though, because I definitely saw the sides of her mouth twitch a few times.

In later years, these control rooms were shut down and a large call centre control room opened at Headquarters. This was manned mainly by civilians or Police support staff, which is the correct terminology these days. I fully understood the reason behind such moves, but by God, we lost a lot of common sense deployment, as the new system did not incorporate all the local knowledge, because by then, there was none. Redditch, for instance, was controlled from HQ by someone who had no connection to the place, little or no knowledge of local crime trends and certainly no experience in managing incidents or using the correct deployments. At least the local controller of his or her day was able to deploy resources to various points, to try and cut off the escape routes of the travelling criminal, and all that was lost. They called it progress and they said change was good, but I, like many others of my time, did not entirely agree with it. Change often took the fun out of life.

My time as a Controller lasted from 1986 to 1988 on and off. In the late part of 1987 and early part of 1988 I was placed on acting Sergeant duties. I had been getting some favourable appraisals, and we had a Chief Superintendent who was very approachable, and who always came and sat with us for a cup of tea in the control room on a Sunday Morning. His name was Brian Humphries. I often used to drop hints that I was looking to move on to the next rank. He was the sort of gaffer in whose company you could relax, and he always had time for the lower ranks, not like some gaffers I had the misfortune to meet.

The Sub-Divisional Superintendent was Alan Poulton (RIP), another very approachable man, and one I had a lot of respect for. In an appraisal he told me he had been getting some good comments about my time in the control room, not, by the way, about the pranks, which hopefully he didn't get to know about, but about their confidence in leaving me to manage incidents effectively. He offered me an acting role and said this was my chance to prove myself in the next rank, and if I did not mess up, he would support me.

I was put to work with other shifts over the next twelve months, covering Substantive Sergeants, who were either away on leave, or on courses or long-term sick. I was shadowing other Substantive Sergeants, one or two of them who had been Constables with me, such as Gareth. Gareth was a Constable in Wellington when I first joined, and he had about three months more service than me. They were all very supportive of me and gave me the encouragement to go for the promotion boards.

As I mentioned at the start of this book, I was the type of character who was either liked or hated. I could come across sometimes as abrupt, and say the wrong things to those who didn't really know me. I had a tendency to speak my mind and give my opinions, which didn't always go down well with some people. While I was a Controller I would often assert my authority over the radio if someone argued about certain deployments. The Shift Inspector or Sergeant would say to me,

"You have our authority to deploy as you see fit." I think some saw me as having the short man syndrome, and I suppose they thought I could be more tactful. Looking back to those days, as a much older and wiser man, I could see their point, and in truth, my wife often told me I could be abrupt with people.

I eventually went for the promotion boards in the latter part of 1987. There were two boards to get through, the first was the preliminary, an interview with a high-ranking Officer such as a Chief Superintendent, and an Inspector with a Sergeant. If you passed that, you were then selected for the central board, involving the Chief Constable, one of his assistant Chief Constables, and normally your Divisional Superintendent, in my case Mr Humphries. Mr Humphries didn't normally ask any questions; he was there to speak to the Chief while you waited outside. The Chief at the time was Mr Mullett (RIP).

My central board took place just after the Hungerford shooting massacre in August 1987. This was about an armed man wandering the streets of Hungerford, aimlessly shooting people dead. I was asked what I would do if I was the Duty Sergeant at Bromsgrove, and a report came in of a gunman on the loose in a part of Bromsgrove. Now, at that time it was clear that what happened in Hungerford was that unarmed Police went into the area and were shot. Other members of the public had also been shot. In those days, there were no armed response cars. Normally only Authorised Shots, ie those authorised to carry guns, were called in.

In those days, Authorised Shots were ordinary day-to-day Officers. They could be Detectives, Traffic Officers, or beat Officers. These Officers attended refresher courses to maintain their skills. I remember that HQ had a list of those available, and if any incident kicked off, they would be called in. A bit like the RNLI, I suppose, when needed they would drop everything and come and pick up their weapon. The armory, as I recall, was at Divisional Headquarters.

I remember on my newly promoted Sergeants Course back in 1988, at West Midlands Tally Ho School, we had a lecture from the West Midlands Firearms Unit. They were one of the first Forces to set up a dedicated full time Firearms Unit. West Mercia followed suit with the Task Force, and all this came about because of Hungerford, I believe. We were shown an old news clip of a firearm siege somewhere in the UK, and it was so unreal that it was funny.

It was a residential street, and the news clip showed a uniformed Policeman, with his helmet on, lying on the floor with a rifle pointing at the house where the suspect was. There was a low wall bordering the property and there were a couple of other uniformed Officers crouched below the wall with pistols. To top it all, the TV cameras were a little further back behind the Officer lying on the floor, and members of the public in the street to the left, watching what was going on. There was no cordon, and they were all exposed. The news footage was from the fifties or perhaps a little later. I'm glad to say things have moved on somewhat.

Anyway, back to my board interview. Without much thinking, I told them the first thing I would do was to notify the Force Control Room Inspector, and request the deployment of the fairly newly-formed air unit, and inform all patrols to make for the general area, but not to approach the gunman. I was then asked,

"So, you are prepared to allow a gunman to roam the streets?" I stood my ground and pointed out to the panel that in Hungerford, Police Officers had been shot for going straight in. It would be no good having dead Officers lying around, and then I came out with a flippant remark to Mr Mullet,

"Would you allow Officers into a danger area such as that?" Eyebrows were raised at that comment. I continued,

"The area would need to be contained, and a strategy set up. As a Sergeant, I would not be making the big decisions about deployment."

"Oh dear," I thought, "I have blown it." I had thrown a question back at the Chief Constable, Mr Mullett. I thought I'd better get my coat and get back to walking the beat for the next few years. There was a short silence in the room, and Mr Mullett looked on blankly. If this had been the old Chief Constable, Mr Rennie, I think I would have been transferred to the far end of the Force at Wem, and demoted to a traffic warden. After about thirty minutes they asked me to wait outside. I was called back in and given the news that I had been successful, and I would be put onto the selection list for promotion. I was not expecting that decision, I can tell you. That was one of the proudest moments of my career, and I harked back to the days when certain members of my family, and in particular, my father-in-law, kept telling me I hadn't got what it took. I was debriefed by Mr Humphries, and he commented on the moment when I had challenged the Chief about the Hungerford event. While waiting outside, the Chief had apparently made mention of the fact that I had challenged him, and the assistant next to him commented to the Chief that he had found me a breath of fresh air.

I went home and broke the news to Anne. I had no idea when or where I would be promoted, but Anne and I discussed the possibilities of having to move away to anywhere in the Force area. Our son, Paul was eleven years old, and had just started senior school, and we were keen for him not to be messed about. Anne was not keen to move far, and certainly did not want to be too far away from her mother, whose MS had now got worse.

I knew there were about seventeen of us on the new promotion list, so it could take up to twelve months before I got the call. I actually got promoted in March 1989, I had turned down one promotion to Shrewsbury, due to the distance involved, and I used Anne's Mom as a lever. Up to the time of my promotion, I more or less continued as an Acting Sergeant at Redditch, sometimes in the control room, and also on a shift. In fact, another promotion board took place before I got promoted, so I was one of the last on my board to get made up. When that day came, Anne sewed my stripes onto my tunic, I fixed the metal Sergeant stripes onto my epaulette, put on my uniform and stood in front of the mirror with a big grin on my face.

This was it, a Substantive rank of Sergeant and a bigger pension payment in the future. I was also mindful that they could quickly be taken away if I messed up.

CHAPTER NINE
NEW SERGEANT, NEW STATION

I had the call at home one day in March 1989, when I was told I was being promoted to Kidderminster, it was not negotiable, and I would be starting the next Monday. I was asked if I required a Police house. I discussed it with Anne and we decided we would stay put and I would travel daily to Kidderminster, which was about a forty-mile round trip. I was assigned to a shift where the shift Inspector was Colin, from the early Wythall days (the Valerie Brown Murder), a recently promoted Sergeant from Redditch who I knew well, and my fellow shift Sergeant was Pat, a newly promoted Constable, also from Redditch. Pat appeared on the boards after mine and he was therefore promoted fairly quickly a few weeks before me.

There was now a situation where a bunch of newly promoted men were moving from B Division at Redditch to a shift at A Division at Kidderminster. In a few years' time, in 2003 in fact, Redditch Division and Kidderminster would become one, and the Command Team would move to Kidderminster. This was the start of the demise for Redditch Police station.

There was, to some extent, some rivalry between Divisions, and obviously, when you find out you are having a new supervisor coming onto your shift, there are those who want to know your reputation. Different Divisions had their own way of doing things, and no one likes change. In a way, it's sort of territorial, and your own Dvision is better than others. Certainly, they don't like new brooms coming in, and anyone upsetting the apple cart and making changes for the sake of it. I was aware back then that I wasn't instantly likeable to everyone. I was the last of the new supervisors on the shift, and I suspect someone had probably done some research, and my somewhat unorthodox reputation had gone before me. In some respects, I was going to have to start again in gaining some respect from the new people I was about to work with.

My first day was on a Monday on nights. I was somewhat apprehensive, nervous and excited at this new venture. I now wore stripes and I was a Substantive Sergeant. I knew very little about Kidderminster, its people, or the town, as it was a place I had hardly ever been to. The satellite villages of Hagley up towards

Birmingham, and Chaddesley Corbett were part of the area. The next town of Stourport on Severn was also in A Division, but was a separate Sub-Division in a similar way to what Bromsgrove was to Redditch. On arrival, I met up with Colin and Pat, before we entered the parade room, for me to meet the men and women who I was going to be supervising and working with. There was about the same number of personnel per shift as there was at Redditch, and that's about twelve or so.

I remember Terry, the shift fast response driver, Rosie (I can't recall her surname), Derek, Trevor, Dave (RIP), Jim and Nadine, to name a few.

My time at Kidderminster would last until November 1991. The station was a close-knit station, and it had a large, very active Members' Club, which used to put on shows. I would go as far as to say it was as big as HQ Club. It wasn't long before I realised the Station was a much more established and happier community than Redditch. It had a feel of pride and loyalty. A lot of the staff there were close and all got on well with each other. I felt like an outsider. Having worked at Redditch for all those years, I was used to the way we worked there, and I needed to adapt to the ways at Kidderminster. Because it was what I was familiar and comfortable with, I tried to impose the ways we had worked in Redditch, on the staff, which. did not go down well with certain members of the shift.

Derek and I did not hit it off at the beginning. Derek was in a way like me, a short man, and our personalities clashed pretty much from the start. As a new Sergeant, I was the patrol Sergeant and within a few days I was taking the parade. This is the start of the shift, where we all meet in the parade room and the shift are allocated their beats and refreshment times. In the old days, the parade meeting involved Constables standing to attention, dressed in full uniform and this gave the Inspector the opportunity to inspect them, and sometimes to find fault. That was all very disciplined. It was nothing like that in 1991, but the parade was still part of the ritual, and Constables were expected to be ready for duty and correctly dressed. As the Sergeant, it was my job to maintain some form of dress and protocol and discipline.

Derek was a smoker, and apparently, prior to my arrival it was not unusual for him to sit and smoke during the parade. Now, I was a smoker myself in those days. I took the attitude that the parade was a ritual that all shifts and all stations up and down the land followed. I did not find smoking on parade acceptable. I suspect he had heard about me from my time in Redditch. During parade, he lit up a cigarette and I asked him not to, so he made snide comments, and others giggled at them. I suppose he was pushing to see how far I would go. It got to a point where I had to take him to task in a room on our own and have a frank discussion.

Colin and Pat were not much help. They knew of this clash and told me I had to sort my differences out with him. We did eventually, it took some months, and it was a battle of the wills, both of us being similar characters. I could be bolshie, as could Derek, I had an abrasive nature and so did he. It took a few months, but we soon buried our differences and I would like to think we became friends; I think we did. Later on, I often went on patrol with Derek, and I began to like his company. He had a similar sense of humour to me, and in years to come, he moved onto the air unit at Halfpenny Green Airport, and I went up in the helicopter with him a couple of times.

In my time at Kidderminster, there was one night that sticks out that was probably the worst for me, which involved the arrest of two on-duty serving Police Officers, not from West Mercia, but from West Midlands. I had only been promoted for a few weeks, and it might have been my second set of nights. I had not yet been trained on the Lion Intoximeter machine. This is the device which measures the alcohol content in the breath when someone is brought into the station for drink driving offences. Colin was trained, but I was not. On this night, for some reason, Pat was away, I am not sure doing what. Dave was an up-and-coming senior Officer in the making, and he was on the shift, working as an Acting Sergeant. There was a dedicated Custody Sergeant on duty, but he finished around midnight, and one of the shift Sergeants then took over the Custody Officer role. I teamed up with Terry in the fast response car. Terry was about my age, he had years of experience and he was a good Police Officer.

He was as straight as they came, dedicated and proud to be an Officer. He held no favours with anyone, and was as honest as could be.

I was still getting to know my shift, and as we cruised the streets of Kidderminster, we were chatting about things in general. It was around midnight and we were following a Mini Metro. Terry told me that he was going to pull the car over, as it was going slightly above the speed limit, and the manner of the driving was not up to his standard. Traffic Officers were a different breed, they had a way of knowing when something wasn't right, and Terry was no exception. They were immovable, had heard all the excuses under the sun, and they would even nick their own mother riding a pedal cycle without lights, and that's during the day! Terry overtook the car, put on the blue lights and when we stopped, he got out.

Not wishing to cramp his style, I remained in the car. He returned with its driver and put him into the back of the Police car. He was a youngish man, about thirty years old.

Terry then asked for a private word, and I stepped outside. He told me the car he had just stopped was a West Midlands Police CID car and in the car, were two on-duty CID officers. He said the car reeked of booze, its passenger was intoxicated and he suspected the driver was too. He told me that he felt this was an accident waiting to happen, and he intended to breath-test the driver. I think Terry was sounding me out, and was in a dilemma about whether he should or he shouldn't. I had never been in a situation like this before, and I told Terry he had to do his job, and do what he felt was the right thing. It matters not really if the man was a Police Officer, we were not above the law. The driver was a Detective Constable and his passenger was his supervisor, a Detective Sergeant. They were both from the Dudley/Black Country area of the West Midlands Police.

The Constable was respectful and polite, and explained they had been in Kidderminster meeting informants, or making some sort of enquiry, and were making their way back to their station. He was breath-tested, and it was positive, so Terry arrested him. I had to call Colin on the radio and discreetly tell him we were on our way back, and needed to speak to him urgently, because the fact was that he was the only one who could operate the equipment. I did not let on over the radio who the prisoner was. Terry asked that I drive the Mini Metro back to the Station, the Officer gave me his keys and I got into the car. The Sergeant passenger asked what was going on. He was older than the Constable, and he was slurring his words and obviously drunk.

I explained that his driver had been arrested for drink driving and I was taking the car into the station. The passenger then told me they were Police Officers and he had never heard anything like it. He was suggesting we were all in the same job, and this sort of thing wouldn't happen in the West Midlands. I said that procedure had to be followed, and I suggested if he had any concerns, he should speak to my Inspector when we got back. I put the Sergeant into the public office area of the front office. Terry had taken the Constable into the cell block, and put him into a side room while we briefed Colin. This was a first for Colin as well, and we had to start the process. By now, word had spread around the shift that an on-duty Officer had been arrested. The

Station procedure went ahead and the Constable was over the limit, which meant he had to be charged with the offence. The Constable was not placed in a cell, and we did maintain his dignity. He remained courteous, and fully understood what was happening. I could imagine what was going on in his head, his career flashing before him, and what the consequences might be.

Meanwhile, back in the front office the Detective Sergeant was becoming agitated, and kept ringing the bell. Colin went to speak to him, and informed him that his Constable had been arrested. The Sergeant became even more agitated and started making remarks about us all, and, in short, became unprofessional. Colin suggested he calm down and sober up. Colin had also been in touch with the Duty Inspector at Dudley area and appraised him of the situation. The Duty Inspector at West Midlands was told that their car was impounded, and also that his Detective Sergeant was becoming unprofessional.

It was agreed that Dave Jones and I would take the prisoner back to Dudley, and drop him off to the Duty Inspector, which we did. The journey there was a little awkward, and

I found myself apologising to the Detective Constable. He remained courteous and told me there was no need to apologise, and it all remained very calm and professional.

I felt a little sorry for him in a way, he was nothing like his supervisor, who was being an arse back at Kidderminster.

On arrival at Dudley/Black Country we met the Duty Inspector and I briefed him as to the events. He apologised and fully understood we were only doing what any proper upstanding Officer would do. He said he would arrange for a crew to drive to Kidderminster to pick up the Detective Sergeant. With that, I picked up the phone and informed Colin that a West Midlands crew were coming to Kidderminster to collect him. Colin said not to bother, because he'd arrested the detective for disorderly conduct in a Police Station, and had banged him up in a cell. Just when I thought things couldn't get any worse. I informed the Inspector at Dudley, who then had to call the Duty Detective Superintendent at West Midlands and tell him of the evening's event. The time was now about two o'clock in the morning. Meanwhile, Colin had informed our Divisional Superintendent, Peter Picken, who decided to come to the station. Dave and I drove back to Kidderminster and I had to take on the role of Custody Sergeant, and the Detective Sergeant was in a cell, shouting and being generally a pain in the arse.

A West Midlands Superintendent arrived, as did Mr Picken. Both Superintendents went into the cell to speak to the Detective Sergeant. The Sergeant was released into his Superintendent's custody without charge. The Detective Superintendent was clearly embarrassed, and thanked us for the professional way we had dealt with it. All of us involved had to put in detailed reports, and we were later interviewed by West Midlands Police discipline department. Some time later, there was a discipline hearing at West Midlands involving both Officers.

The Detective Constable had appeared in court and was convicted of the offence of drink driving, but he kept his job (Which can't happen anymore, regardless of circumstances). His supervisor, the Sergeant, was sacked. A sorry affair. The Detective Sergeant had acted unprofessionally, when he was a rank above the Detective Constable, and should have shown leadership, and conducted himself professionally. Instead, the Detective Sergeant decided to get drunk, and who knows, maybe the Detective Constable was put in a position where he did what his supervisor told him. I was glad he kept his job and I was a little pleased that the Detective Sergeant lost his as his behaviour on that night was appalling.

Terry had done nothing wrong, but there were some on the CID at Kidderminster who decided that Terry should have turned a blind eye that night. Terry was the subject of some unfavourable comments for the actions he took. There were some with the attitude that Police Officers should look after their own. That's all very well and good for such things as a defective headlight, or driving slightly over the speed limit, but drink driving? I think not. Where do you draw the line? Terry did not let these people get him down, and he continued to be professional, going on to finish his service with distinction.

I spent some time acting as Custody Sergeant at Kidderminster. The role of Custody Sergeant is the only role in the Police Service that is legislated for. The Police and Criminal

Evidence Act 1984 (PACE) created the role. PACE was a big game changer for the Police service, especially the way in which suspects were interviewed, and the rules that came along with it. PACE also introduced the CODES of PRACTICE, a substantial set of rules. Every Officer was given a set of the codes in a paperback book. As a Custody Sergeant, it was essential that I study it and took in the most important parts that related to me. These codes would be used against any officer falling foul of the professional standards. I know a lot of officers would browse through them, then chuck them in the back of a drawer, and never look at them again.

The custody Sergeant has a very heavy responsibility. He or she has responsibility for the care of, and procedures relating to, prisoners in their care. They are not involved in the investigations and are there to see that the prisoners' rights and needs are respected. Records of their time in custody are kept, and scrutinised should there be any complaints, and if anything is not correct, it is the custody sergeant who faces the consequences. Cases can be lost in any court trial if the correct procedures are not adhered to.

One afternoon I was the duty custody officer. We were using the cell block at Stourport, as Kidderminster's block was being refurbished. A husband and wife were brought into me, both accused of shoplifting. They were older than me, I would put them possibly in their fifties. There was no support staff back then employed as Custody assistants, the Custody Sergeant was on his own. He might request the help of a Constable from the Patrol Sergeant if things got busy, but that would depend on the resources available. The two prisoners were separated, to stop them talking to each other, which was normal, the idea being that they would be interviewed separately. The arresting Officers outlined to me the circumstances of their arrests, and I authorised their detention so we could interview them.

The male prisoner protested his innocence from the start, and was quite vocal. He was placed into a cell, as was his wife, while the interviewing Officer prepared the evidence from the witnesses. The man kept pressing the buzzer, wanting to be released, and when that didn't persuade me, he then continually called out. After about an hour he shouted that he did not feel well. His wife had by now gone into her interview. I asked why he felt unwell, and he said he had chest pains, and wanted a doctor. Now it's not unusual for prisoners to try and get out, and use all the excuses under the sun to wrongfoot Custody Sergeants. I also know that you cannot ignore things like this. It may well be that he was trying to pull a fast one, but I was not a doctor. As soon as he told me he had chest pains, I decided to call an ambulance. I may have thought he was trying it on, and I seem to remember I may have allocated a Constable to travel with him in the ambulance to Kidderminster Hospital.

The facts were recorded into his custody record, and off he went in an ambulance, and was well enough at that point to walk into the ambulance. About an hour later his wife had returned to her cell, following her interview, and was informed that her husband had been taken to hospital. Then Pat Herlihy walked into the custody block and informed me that the man had died while in A & E. It was a complete shock to me, because I was convinced he had been making the whole thing up. The cell was sealed off and an enquiry launched. It was decided that the case did not meet the criteria of a death in Police Custody, as he was still alive when he arrived at hospital.

He had indeed died of a heart attack, and apart from having to put in a detailed report, I heard no more about it. Had I ignored the complaints of illness from this man, I don't think I would have been a Sergeant for long. A valuable lesson learned that day and I would never ignore complaints of illness in the future, even though it may be obvious they were trying it on.

I was never entirely happy working at Kidderminster, it was a close-knit station, and many of the Officers there were long standing colleagues. I always felt a bit of an outsider, with not living there, and the fact I was from the rival B Division. It was while I was working at Kidderminster that I had another accident in a Police car. It was a busy night, it was probably around midnight, and the accident was down to my reversing again. I was alone in the marked patrol car, and I was the night Patrol Sergeant. I had just turned off the ring road onto a side road, and I was passing a group of people. A couple of men thought it would be funny to shout some obscenities towards the Police vehicle as it passed. Well that's like a red rag to a bull, so I slammed on the brake, selected reverse and began to reverse, not realizing that a member of the public in his car had also just turned off the ring road into the same side road. BANG, yes you guessed it, I reversed into the front of their car. It was only a low impact collision, but enough to cause a bit of damage to both cars. As for the boys who shouted at me, they ran off, laughing at my demise.

Once again, my reversing skills had let me down, and again Inspector Colin had to attend, and deal with the accident. Luckily, I was not suspended on this occasion, and it all went away, and I was not even sent on a refresher course.

After twelve months at Kidderminster I asked for a transfer back to B Division. I was tired of the travelling every day, and eventually I was told I could go, and in November 1990 I was posted to Rubery on the Bromsgrove Sub-Division.

CHAPTER TEN
RUBERY

Rubery is an outpost Station right on the border with West Midlands Police, and the Station was located on New Road. Towards Birmingham was the county boundary, that's how close we were. To the left was Bromsgrove town, some seven miles or so away. Bromsgrove was the mother Station and where we took our prisoners.

The Station was old and was due to be demolished, and a new one built, which did happen in the early nineties. There were four shifts and one Sergeant to each shift, and one Inspector.

Rubery covered a patch from the border with Longbridge, and it encompassed Frankley, a large housing estate of both private and council property. Frankley was an overspill area of Birmingham, and the housing sat just inside the area of Worcestershire, but in term of its residents, they were mainly Birmingham people. To the people that lived there, they were Brummies, and had no real allegiance to Worcestershire.

In 1995 as part of the Boundary

Commissions review, Frankley was transferred back to Birmingham City Council, and as a consequence West Midlands Police took over the Policing of the area.

In one way, we were glad to see the back of Frankley. It had some nasty, bad people living there, but on the other hand it was a good learning place for new Officers, and once we lost it, Rubery was downgraded and became a quieter area to work.

My move to Rubery and up to retirement was my most enjoyable time. This period up to my retirement gave me job satisfaction, and it was a privilege to carry the office of Constable, although I was a Sergeant. I was destined to be in this rank for the remainder of my service. I had taken the Inspector's exam twice, but failed on one paper. There were some good laughs and good teamwork as well. The people I would come to work with were all good people, some of whom I still see now and then at the odd reunion, or just to catch up with them, and of course there is social media.

In Policing terms, we were basically an extension of the Greater Birmingham area, as the boundary was just an invisible line, one property would come under West Mercia and the property next door could be West Midlands. One side of the street would be West Mercia and the other West Mids. The area of Wythall a similar out-station was to the north east, and bordered the Maypole and Kings Heath area. This was a sister station and, like Rubery, was within the Bromsgrove District. We very often covered Wythall patch if the Officers from there were committed, or dealing with a prisoner, and if we had to do a blue light run, from Rubery to Wythall, the route would take us through Longbridge and Kings Norton to get to Wythall. These areas are in the West Midlands area.

Rubery was an exciting area to work. Apart from the council areas of Frankley, we also took in the area of Barnt Green, an exclusive area which attracted the rich and famous. Members of the pop group UB40 lived there, as did Ron Atkinson of football fame, as well as other footballers and business people. But the most famous person of all was Paul Henry, better known as Benny from crossroads. Barnt Green sat with in the Lickey Hills, a well-known beauty spot on the border. The travelling criminal was attracted to places like Barnt

Green, and to Blackwell, next to Barnt Green. Vehicle crime was an ongoing problem at the Lickey Hills. There was certainly a mixture of all types of Police work that kept us busy, from thefts and domestics on the Frankley, to dwelling house burglaries and high value car thefts in Barnt Green.

Some of the people I had the pleasure of working with were Andy, Inspector David Shaw (not the David who became the Chief in later years, he was from West Midlands), Hilary, Mark O C, Vince, Lee, Paul aka (Knocker), Tony, Mark (aka Big Bird) to name a few. During my time at Rubery the building was demolished, and we moved into an old shop along the High Street for about 18 months, and then moved into the new modern Station. I don't intend to write about the incidents I attended, because there were too many to mention, but some do stick out in my mind. I probably dealt with, or was involved in, the more serious stuff while at Rubery.

In towns like Redditch and Kidderminster, crime was committed mainly by the criminals of that town, but for places like Rubery and Wythall, the majority of crime was committed by criminals from outside the area, so a lot of our work and arrest took place in the West Midlands area. We had a couple of established Special Constables who worked out of Rubery. One was Kevin Bird and the other Alex. Both were mature men; Kevin was very popular, but Alex not so much with some people. Kevin lived on the Frankley estate. One night in the early hours, Kevin, who was off-duty, heard a domestic dispute with his next door neighbours. He could hear them shouting and screaming, and he was that concerned he called 999.

I was out that night with Andy, one of the Constables on the shift. We had another double crew on with us that night, and we all responded. Andy and I got there first to find the front door to the premises open, and we could see Kevin struggling and fighting with a man in the hallway of his neighbour's house. There was a heavy smell of petrol in the air and we soon established that the man had doused the house in petrol. There was a woman in there and the man was attempting to strike matches, and Kevin was fighting with him, trying to stop him setting fire to the house. What Kevin was doing was very brave and were it not for him, there would have been a serious incident, and possibly serious injury, or worse, for someone. Andy and I went in and between the three of us, we managed to overpower this man and get him cuffed. The other crew arrived and took him away.

Prior to our arrival, Kevin had heard the woman screaming the words

"He is trying to kill me," and Kev had taken it upon himself to smash the front door in, to be faced with the smell of petrol, and the man attempting to ignite the place.

I submitted a report about Kevin's actions and he received a Chief Constable's award. Andy and I got naff all, but then again, it wasn't about us. I just felt Kevin needed to be recognised for his actions. I was never one to blow my own trumpet, I was never one to go looking for rewards or things of that nature, but it is nice, though, at times to be given a pat on the back, and to be acknowledged by higher ranks for having done a good job.

I never received any Chief Constable awards, but I did get two Divisional ones, and one of these was while I worked at Rubery. It was a dark night during the winter. A young mother had been reported missing from the Blackwell area.

She had been suffering from depression and she was suicidal. Her family had reported her missing and feared she was going to kill herself. I attended the address with one of my shift, but at the moment I cannot recall who. I took the report seriously and at the rear of the property ran the main railway line from Birmingham to the west Country, trains travelling at regular intervals at speeds of up to ninety miles an hour. My gut reaction was that she could be on the tracks, and there was no other basis for this thought, other than a gut feeling. I radioed into control and asked that they immediately contact British Transport Police to put a caution on the line.

My knowledge of my days of employment on the railways was kicking in. Putting a caution on the line means the drivers of any train must drive at a reduced speed, and this is done by putting the signals at a single yellow.

I then asked for the air unit to be deployed and to do a sweep of the railway line from Barnt Green towards Bromsgrove. It was dark and if she had been on the line, she could be walking and making progress. I asked for dog handlers to come to the area. The air unit arrived after about twenty minutes, and we could see the helicopter's navigation lights in the sky. The helicopter had heat source cameras, and within a couple of minutes of it arriving, they found a heat source at the side of the track, but the heat source was not confirmed as being a human. We had to go down a steep incline, then climb over a high fence to get onto the side of the track. In those days, we did not have high viz clothing, it was pitch black and all we had were our torches.

Although I had asked for trains to be put on a caution, I had no way of knowing if that had been implemented, and I had to quickly advise my colleague to remain to the left, away from the track as much as possible, and should he hear an approaching train, to get down or lie down, till it had passed. This was because a high-speed train passing close by could suck you in.

The air unit could see us on their thermal image camera, and talked us in to the heat source, and there we found the vulnerable woman. She was distressed, sitting on the rail, crying. We managed to coax her away and escort her to safety, and a passing train came within two minutes of us finding her, and there is little doubt that we saved her life. Other Officers at the top of the bank assisted us, and as I recall she was taken away in an ambulance. I never did find out what happened to her in the end, and I never heard from the family, although I understand they were very grateful. It was reported to the Sub-Divisional Superintendent and my colleague and I were given a Divisional commendation. My second commendation came years later, but I will write about that in a later chapter.

During my time at Rubery, I very often had to cover supervisory duties at Bromsgrove. There was only one Sergeant on each shift at Rubery, but there were two each shift at Bromsgrove, these being the Custody Sergeant and a Patrol Sergeant. The shift at Bromsgrove was our sister shift and our back-up.

Bromsgrove had a control room and a Controller. The Sub-Divisional fast response car worked out of that Station, and covered the whole Sub-Division of Bromsgrove, taking in Rubery and Wythall area.

Now, I mentioned earlier about practical

jokes and having a laugh. This next scenario still gets talked about at reunions. I can't remember the year, but it was a night duty which started at ten in the evening and finished at six in the morning.

On nights, the fast response crew would always come to Rubery at two am for their refreshment break. The crew was Paul (Knocker) and, I believe, Tony. Paul was a long-standing traffic-orientated Officer, and this is what he specialised in. The fast response crew were a general crew, but most were from the ex-traffic department, which had been demobbed, so to speak, and put back as a Divisional resource. This just left the motorway crews for the most part under the remit of HQ.

Paul had years of experience, and Tony a few years less. On this particular night, I was covering Patrol Sergeant for the Sub-Division, because the Patrol Sergeant at Bromsgrove was on leave. The Custody Sergeant was Alan, a long-established character, a bit long in the tooth, with not long left before he retired. He was also known for having a sense of humour.

The Controller that night was Jan, a tall lady, with a cutting tongue, in the comical sense. She could shoot a man down with one lash of her tongue, and a great girl to have a laugh with. She could dish it out as well as take it.

Unbeknown to me, earlier in the night at around midnight, Paul had asked if he could finish duty at two am, providing it was quiet. He had asked Jan, and she spoke to Alan, and between them they intended to let him have the time off. But as a joke, Alan told Jan to tell Paul he could not, as someone had just been arrested in Newquay in Cornwall, over two hundred miles away.

The story was that he'd been arrested on a Bromsgrove court warrant, and Paul might have to go to Newquay with Tony to pick him up.

She had even produced a fake telex message purporting to be from Devon and Cornwall Police, with a fictitious name of the prisoner on. Now this is normal practice across the UK. If someone is wanted by one Force area and they are arrested in another Force area, then you have to go and fetch them. Jan relayed to Paul the fact that he may have to go to Newquay, but then forgot to tell him it was a joke. She became busy and Alan had prisoners, so the matter was forgotten. Of course, there was no prisoner in Newquay and there never was.

Two o'clock came and went. I was in the station at Rubery, having my break, and at half past two, Paul and Tony had not come in. I called the control and asked where the pair were as they had not arrived for their break. I could hear Jan calling them on the radio, but she was getting no response, so I asked if they'd been sent to any incidents, and if so, I wanted to know where and that they were okay. Jan said she would call me on the landline, which is always a sign that something is wrong and it is something not to be aired over the radio.

"I think they may be on their way to Newquay," she quipped.

"Why?" I said. She then relayed the story to me about Paul wanting time off, and the rest of it, and that she had forgotten to tell them it was a joke. She did not think that they would actually go to Newquay.

"How long ago was this?" I asked.

"About two hours ago," she said. That meant they were possibly more than half way to Newquay.

"Jan, can you give the crew a call on the

VHF radio system?"

"No dice," she came back after a few minutes of trying. Mobile phones were not around in those days in the way they are today.

"Right, Jan, phone Newquay and explain that two West Mercia Officers might turn up there." By this time, we knew they'd gone, and we couldn't get them back.

I got a phone call at about four in the morning from Paul. He was indeed in Newquay Police Station, and told me about his arrival. He got there after we'd warned Newquay they were on their way. Paul and Tony had arrived and parked up, and walked into the front office at Newquay. They introduced themselves and said they had come to pick up a prisoner.

"What prisoner? There isn't any prisoner," said the Constable on the front office, no doubt in a Cornish accent.

The penny dropped then, and Paul and Tony realised they'd been the victims of a Jan and Alan joke that had just backfired. To add insult to injury, the Newquay Officer posed a riddle to Paul. He asked, "What's the difference between a photograph and a West Mercia Officer?"

"Don't know," came the reply.

"A photograph is developed," said the Newquay Officer. Not much of a punchline, in fact not much of a joke, but he probably thought it was funny.

"Paul, I swear I knew nothing about this prank," I said to him over the phone. "We've been trying to get hold of you, and hoped we'd get you before you got there." Apparently, they'd driven there at high speed and came back at a sedate speed, arriving back late morning, intending to claim the overtime.

Jan and Alan had to pay money out of their own pockets for the cost of the fuel, and had a telling off from the Superintendent.

There was a lot of joviality during my time at Rubery. I remember one occasion when we were housed in the temporary Police Station at the shop. We had access to the rear where we parked our personal cars and Police cars. Andy was a major piss-taker, he used to say, and still does say, that he suffers from Sarcasm Tourette's Syndrome. He liked taking the mickey, but he was always good-natured when he was on the receiving end as well.

Mark (Big Bird) was always the butt of jokes. Mind you, he could dish it out too. He was another one who could take a joke when it was on him. I remember one joke Andy played on Mark. It was about six o'clock one morning, and Mark was going home. Mark liked to play music in his car, but at very high volume, and I used to dread to think just what it would be like inside his car. He wouldn't have heard a thing from outside the car when he was driving.

Andy thought it would be funny to tie a metal bucket to the back of Mark's car and see how long it took him to realise he was towing the bucket up the road. Mark O'C was there also. We watched as he drove out from the back of the shop towards the High Street, and we all laughed when we saw the bucket clanging and bouncing on the road behind him. Mark did not realise, of course, because he had his music on. Once he turned onto the High Street, he would drive about half a mile where he would then join the main A38 dual carriageway towards Bromsgrove, a 70 MPH road. Realising he was unaware of the bucket, Andy and Mark O'C had to quickly jump into a Police car and race after him to stop him before he reached the dual carriageway. It was such a funny sight.

Luckily, they managed to get to him before he was anywhere near the main road.

Some readers will say this type of prank is irresponsible, and they would probably be right, but back then it was part of the ritual, and there was no harm done. The nature of the job could be stressful, and this was a way of letting off steam. The humour helped to keep up morale, and the camaraderie was important to maintain a happy and hardworking team.

Snow at night time was another let-your-hair-down moment, and, of course, there were snowball fights. I remember one occasion, Mark (Big Bird) again involved, during the early hours of the morning. We had deep snow and we were out on the Frankley somewhere. I was with Andy, Mark was with a colleague, and we'd been throwing snow balls at each other. Mark ran back to his Police car, locked his door and started shouting obscenities at us. He thought he was safe with his door locked.

Unfortunately for him, the back tailgate was not locked, so we opened it and bombarded him with snowballs as he squealed like a girl, frantically trying to start the car's engine to get away.

I can't leave this part of my story without mentioning the support staff at Rubery, Cath

Smith, Maureen Townsend, Gina Troth and Sheila, our cleaner. They were the lynchpins and mother hens of the station that kept us children in check. Cath, Maureen and Gina were the public face of the station, they worked the front counter, took messages and generally kept the tea and milk stocks up. Sheila was more than a cleaner, she was well known for cooking breakfasts too, so much so the fast response crews would come in from Bromsgrove to get one.

Rubery was a happy Station and one of the best times of my career. When Frankley was transferred to West Midlands, the place became quieter, and the Station was downgraded from a four-Sergeant to a two-Sergeant station. I was one of the two sergeants to remain and Greg was the second. Greg was older than me and had been in the rank for a long time. He was different from me, he didn't have my sense of humour, and his style of supervision was a lot stricter than mine. I was the more popular of the two of us. The Constables still continued on a twenty four-hour shift system. Greg and I alternated between the days, the latest we would work to was midnight, and we started at eight o'clock in the morning. The Constable ratio would drop to about four per shift. Rubery also had its beat Officers, at Barnt Green and Alvechurch. The Alvechurch beat Officer was Dave, known as Mad Robbo. He was a year older than me, and he came to Rubery from Worcester. The Barnt Green Officer was Howard, again about the same age as me, and a likable character, but he could also be irritating at times, as he would constantly be cracking jokes, and I mean bad jokes. Also working out of Rubery was my old mucker, Dick, we had been in the same class at the start at Ryton on Dunsmore, we'd worked together at Redditch, and here he was again with me at Rubery. Robbo and Dick would both follow me to my next posting, which is where we all were when we retired. Retirement is eleven years back down the line now, and we are all still in contact and meet up with each other.

Rubery saw its fair share of serious crime, from armed robberies to serious assaults, to a murder on the Frankly estate. The murder involved a man stabbed outside a pub. Earlier on that year (I can't recall the exact time or year) another victim had been stabbed. The assailant was known to us; in fact, he had a fearsome reputation, and no one in the area would give a statement, so nothing could be proved, but luckily, the victim survived. It was common knowledge who had been responsible, all the Officers in that area knew it was him. In between the first stabbing, the stabbing murder, this same assailant was wanted for other offences.

I recall one incident where he was seen on the Frankley, and Vince, a large-built, extremely fit officer, a transferee from the Metropolitan Police, had given chase, and caught hold of him. He was about to make the arrest, when this assailant told Vince if he didn't let go he would stick him (stab him). He said he had done it before and he would do it again.

I believe this was at night, and in order not to put his life at risk, Vince let go of him, because he couldn't see if he had a knife in his hand or not, and all of us knew he had done it before. The suspect ran off.

On the night of the stabbing, I was the Patrol Sergeant. We all arrived at the scene, where there was a lot of blood from the pedestrian area to the pub. It was after midnight, and an ambulance crew had just taken the victim away on our arrival. There was a crowd around, and some of the women were crying and a little hysterical. We maintained the scene, cleared people back, and cordoned off the area. From what the public was telling us, it sounded and looked serious. Most people were naming the assailant, and it was the same name as in the previous stabbing. We managed to get some names of people as they were walking away. CID were called out, and I think we managed to get one or two statements at the time.

We went straight to an address where we thought we might find the assailant. We went mob-handed, about six of us, but he wasn't there, and he had gone to ground. The victim died from his injuries and a full-scale murder operation began. We gathered a lot of evidence, a team of PSU trained Officers were used each time addresses were visited, in an attempt to arrest the suspect, and he was eventually found. Vince had made a statement about the time he had caught up with him, and in his statement the comments the defendant had made about having stabbed someone before, were clearly recorded, but the judge wouldn't allow Vince's evidence to be used.

I am struggling to remember if he was actually found guilty. I think I recall that the jury found him not guilty, but I also think that there was some witness intimidation as well.

CHAPTER ELEVEN
WYTHALL, SUMMER

It was a hot day. Really hot. Tommy's uniform, and mine, were uncomfortable in the days before air conditioning was installed. Our operation had to be planned and executed carefully if we were going to be successful. Our target was called Lincoln, and he was actually the son of a retired Police Sergeant. I had to keep watch from a lower window while Tommy was struggling to stand on a chair as he looked through a higher window, which was the only one we could open. We watched as our target stripped down to just his shorts and shoes in the excessive heat. He looked around to see if anyone was watching, before inspecting the new petrol lawnmower in front of him. Judging it the best I could to calculate travelling speed and distance to target, I called the strike.

"NOW," I said, hoping I had timed it right.

Tommy performed perfectly, and tipped the bucket of ice-cold water out of the window with pinpoint accuracy to douse the unsuspecting victim below. Scrabbling in rapid retreat to our office, we sat there wearing straight faces. I was pretending to be on an important phone call and Tommy was busy writing a serious report as our dripping wet and shivering handyman squelched back inside, wearing a look of furious horror.

"Oh!" I said, with believable shock "Has it started raining, mate?"

In my view, the service we gave to the public began to slide downhill from 1996. Up until then anyone reporting a crime, more often than not, got a visit from an Officer. The Officer on patrol was sent to Joe Public if they found their car broken into overnight, or their car stolen, or the odd garden ornament pinched, or the milk on the door step taken. Statements were taken and the Officer returned to the Station and filled out a crime report. The Sergeant then viewed the report and issued instructions for the investigating Constable to report back within a week or so on his enquiries. The Constable was expected to knock on neighbours' doors, to try and find any witnesses or any information that might lead to finding the offenders. The Constable wrote his report back to the Sergeant, and it ended up on the desk of the Detective Inspector on CID, who would then either recommend it be filed as undetected, or issue further instructions.

This was about to change in the name of progress. They were starting to set up Crime Desks up across the Force area, and Bromsgrove was next on the list. Some Divisions had already implemented their Crime Desks. A Crime Desk consisted of a Sergeant and a couple of support staff. Admittedly, there were often crimes reported where there was no chance of finding an offender. For example, graffiti appearing overnight in an isolated area, where no one would have been about to witness it. The way a Crime Desk worked was when a member of the public rang in to report a crime, providing it was not happening there and then, the call was put through to the Crime Desk. The Crime Desk took the details over the phone and generated a crime number. Certain questions would be asked of the victim, and if it warranted an attendance by an Officer, the crime was allocated to the area where it happened, and one of the Sergeants on that area would then allocate it to an Officer for investigation and further report.

If the Crime Desk Sergeant decided there were no "legs" in the crime reported, he would file it straightaway as undetected; effectively, this was a screening-out exercise.

A couple of years later, the Crime Desks became the Public Service Desks, and were staffed around the clock, and the PSD (not to be confused with the gestapo PSD!) took all calls from the public, and were not just crime recording. Over the next few years, fewer and fewer jobs were resourced, and much of the crime reported was mainly dealt with over the phone by the PSD, which was made up mostly of support staff, with a Sergeant supervising. Today you will be lucky to get a Police Officer at your door when reporting a crime. Even house burglaries don't get attended until days after. I think the service the Police give today is far worse from my day. It's all down to costs, and political interference. When I joined the service, the Police were seen to be independent of any political connection, and that's how it should be. Today we have Police and Crime Commissioners voted in by the public. Most are from Political Parties, and that cannot be right.

Geoff was the Sergeant at Wythall, and during 1996 he was asked to set up the Crime

Desk which was to be based at Bromsgrove. I was asked to move for two weeks to Wythall, and cover for Geoff while he was carrying out this new venture. I went, as I was asked to, and ended up staying nine years. The move suited me, as I only lived two miles from the Station. It was a one-Sergeant Station and I was pretty well left to my own devices, and to some extent could choose my own hours, which were mainly between eight in the morning and ten at night. I was not classed as a Response Sergeant, I was under the supervision of the Geographic Inspector at Bromsgrove. The role was more community based, sorting out local problems and getting involved with partners such as the Parish Council, local housing and groups. The Constables based at Wythall were expected to be responsive, and also to deal with local issues. When I moved to Wythall the Constables worked a twenty four-hour shift system, but this changed over the years, when the Station was downgraded, and changes made in the way the area was Policed.

Throughout my service there were always changes afoot, depending who the new broom was. A woman Chief Superintendent was at the helm at Redditch, the Divisional HQ for Redditch and Bromsgrove, which included Wythall. Her management team came up with the idea of Sector Policing. This involved renting premises in various parts of the Division, and kitting them out with phones, computers and other essential offices equipment, and placing a Sergeant and a certain number of Officers in these outposts. The Sector then took responsibility for that area, on a community basis, and they weren't a first response to emergency calls. The response team at Redditch took on the responsibility of first response, but the response teams would at times be stretched, as the Officers posted to Sectors were mainly taken away from the response team. Just prior to the set-up of Sector Policing, a certain Chief Superintendent had brought in an outside consultant, to advise her on how to put it in place and manage it. There were a couple of Divisional parades, which were basically a meeting held with all personnel, when we were told what was happening, and there was a Q&A session. The questions had to be submitted first for screening. (Joke).

There were some who were sceptical and

privately critical of the amount of money being spent on this private consultancy firm; public money I would add. What do they know about Policing? That was one common question. In the end she implemented Sector Policing, Wythall was classed as a Sector, and my Constables were not supposed to be reactive to grade A calls. However, they often were, because of the distance from Redditch and Bromsgrove, plus the response teams were always short staffed. At night-time within the Redditch area, at times there were only two cars out after midnight, due to the lack of Officers. On paper, each response team had about six to eight Officers, but with leave and sickness, it sometimes got dangerously low. Another new feature that came from this type of Policing, again concerning night-time incidents, was something that created a degree of ill-feeling at times. In order to keep the response team free, if they were called to an incident they were expected to obtain a complaint statement, gather evidence and leave a written report for the sector to continue the ongoing enquires the next morning, and to deal with any prisoners.

However, this was not always the case, and I put this down to a couple of reasons;

sometimes it might be individual laziness, and on other occasions it might be for operational reasons, such as especially busy times. I would get many a complaint from my Constables at the way things were dealt with during the night. We very often found that nothing had been done when it should have been, and the log would be marked for a Sector Officer to deal with in the morning. My Officers would look to me to see that these things didn't happen in the future. A quick browse on the Operational Information System would tell me if the response crews had been busy during the night, and therefore had a reasonable excuse not to have done what was expected of them. I had a reputation for speaking my mind. If I thought things had not been done correctly, I would say so. I might not have been diplomatic about it, when I needed to get my point across. Like other Sergeants, I was protective of my patch and my Officers, and I was there to support them, and to try to make life as stress-free as possible and to see that a job was done properly. Two incidents spring to mind. In Wythall there was a miscreant I will call John, and I won't say his surname name. He hung around with another miscreant I will call Lee, and, as with John, I won't give his full name.

These two had a reputation around Wythall for being anti-Police and violent. They had their hangers-on, and anyone who crossed them was invariably intimidated. Lee was reputed to carry a machete, and there was a marker on the Police National Computer to this effect. John was older than Lee, and lived with a girl I will call June, and there was a history of an on-off relationship, which was stormy at times and involved domestic violence. This is a true incident, but I have changed their names for obvious reasons.

One Saturday evening, for some reason there was no night cover at Wythall. I think it was at a time when Wythall shut down at two o'clock in the morning, which was the case in my latter years.

A crowd of young men, including John and Lee, had been to a local chip shop, and one of the crowd smashed some items in the shop, this activity all caught on CCTV. The Police were called and the Saturday night Public Order van was dispatched from Redditch. Most of the people in the van were members of the Special Constabulary and one or two regular

Constables.

They seized the CCTV and established that the bloke who'd done this was in a first floor flat somewhere in Wythall, along with John, Lee and some others. The Officers attended the flat and were faced with some resistance. They were refused access, and John and Lee were hurling abuse at them through the windows. Of course, alcohol played a large part, as it usually does. The Constables decided they were going to force entry, which they had the power to do, although whether it was the right decision remained to be seen. An arrestable offence had been committed, and the suspected offender was on the premises, and in order to effect an arrest, the Officers had the power to gain entry, by force if necessary. This was the justification for forcing entry on that night.

There were a couple of shields on the van, and these were used, but of course, the members of the Special Constabulary had no training in the use of shields. The door had been barricaded from the inside, and the Officers forced entry, while items were being hurled at them. Batons had been drawn, and John received a blow to his head from over the top of a shield. Now there was no Sergeant present, and all this took place on the say so of the Constable present, and the Specials went along with it. John was laid out, and removed or dragged down the stairs and taken outside. Meanwhile, the Duty Sergeant for the night, Roger, arrived from Redditch, having been told what was happening. He arrived at the scene to find a prisoner bleeding from a head wound caused by the baton, the flat in disarray and general carnage, with a number of persons arrested.

John was taken to hospital under escort, Lee was taken to the station, and those remaining in the house were spoken to, but refused to co-operate. Oh, and the person responsible for causing the damage to the chip shop had escaped through a back window. His name was known to us, though. Roger was not best pleased at how all this had been handled. The remainder of the night was spent putting together statements, and a report, for the oncoming Officers at Wythall to deal with the next morning.

The prisoner, Lee, was bedded down in the cells for the night, and John taken to hospital, where I believed he was released from Police custody, because the doctor kept him in. We would speak to him at a later date. There were only two Constables on duty at Wythall that next morning, and any plans they had for that day had to wait. I was called at home in the morning to be told what had happened, so I went into work for eight o'clock, and was given a full briefing.

The first job was to go round to the perpetrator's address and arrest him for criminal damage at the chip shop, which was swiftly done, and he was taken to the cells at Redditch. At the hospital, John had been de-arrested, and we planned to see him later. After all the information came in, it transpired John and Lee would only be eligible for an affray charge, not something we would go and arrest for. John turned up at the front door of Wythall Police Station with his solicitor a few days later, after I had been in contact with him. He refused to be interviewed on the advice of his solicitor, so on the doorstep I told him he would be reported for the offence of Affray and I cautioned him. His solicitor sarcastically said,

"This should be fun, we will see you in court."

As it turned out, he did not see me in court because his client pleaded guilty and if my memory serves me right, he was sent down for a month or two.

The second incident that springs to mind also happened during the night. It was another public order situation in the area of Hopwood. Again, a response crew attended, and there were assaults and witnesses. What should have been done, is that statements should have been taken, any evidence obtained, and a brief report made out for the early turn Sector Officer .and all they had done was updated the log for Sector to deal. I arrived at work about nine o'clock that morning, and my early turn Officers told me about the pile of poo left by the response night crew from Redditch. I was angry and when I looked at the log and saw that nothing had been done, in my usual brash style, I began complaining about the response crews in general, calling them lazy bastards, and so forth. This was a typical response from me, engaging mouth before brain, because unbeknown to me there was a couple of response crews in the next room having their morning refreshment break.

Now, what I haven't mentioned here yet is that the response teams came under a female Inspector. I had already had a disagreement with her over a Police vehicle accident involving one of my Officers, which I will come to soon. The two Officers who heard my outburst obviously said something back at Redditch, and this filtered through to this Inspector. She went and saw the Superintendent and Chief Inspector and told them. She did not think to contact me directly and discuss it, so I could point out to her the shortcomings of her Officers from the night before. Within a few days, I was hauled before the Chief Inspector and was told that for the next three months I was being moved to a response shift at Redditch, and to look upon it as being developed. I tried to reason with him and explain that the Officers had not done their job properly, but he was firmly on the side of this Inspector.

So for the next three months, I swapped with another Sergeant and worked on the response shift at Redditch, covering twenty four hours. Now I am not one to hold a grudge, but even today if I should bump into that Chief Inspector I would ask him again why he came to that decision. The C/I in question was pensioned off shortly after this event, due to a bad car accident. Having been suitably developed, I returned to Wythall to resume my previous role of Community Sergeant.

CHAPTER TWELVE
INCIDENTS AND CRASHES

My nine years at Wythall saw many a serious incident. You might be familiar with the murder of Lee Harvey, a man who was stabbed by his girlfriend, Tracy Andrews, in Alvechurch. This case made national headlines, and ran on the news for some time, and is the subject of other TV programmes, mainly those on the satellite channels talking about notorious crimes.

This was, again, something which happened during the night on Wythalls patch, and we arrived at work to find the incident was live and ongoing. HQ had sent a senior Detective, crews from Redditch were at the scene, and apparently, information was being sought. In the early stages, Tracy Andrews claimed that they were chased by a car and Lee was stabbed by someone in that car. We were the community Officers for Alvechurch. Dave (Robbo) was the Alvechurch Officer, and he knew most people there. He, as well as a couple of other Officers, had had dealings with Tracy Andrews and Lee Harvey in the past. Their relationship was a stormy one and Police had been to domestics involving them a number of times.

On the morning of the crime, which had actually taken place in a country lane in the early hours, Dave offered his services to CID, but was told he was not required. At the time the CID were working on the information at hand, and that information was being fed to them by Tracy Andrews, so initially she was not a suspect. This apparent rejection of Dave's offer did not go down well with him, and Dave, who can be stroppy at times, chose not to tell the investigators what he knew of their stormy relationship. Not one person on that enquiry bothered to pick up the phone to me or Dave and ask if there was anything we knew, as local Officers, about the couple, that might help their inquiries. Maybe it was an oversight.

A few days later, after TV news appeals, it transpired that a witness had not been far behind the car being used by Andrews and Lee Harvey, and the evidence from the witness suggested that Andrews had made up the story about a car following them, and the occupants attacking Lee. Tracy Andrews had murdered her boyfriend, she was charged and convicted, even though she denied it all though her trial, only to confess to her crime years into her sentence.

Another overnight incident happened in a country lane called Icknield Street, in Alvechurch, a one-track narrow lane. This area was notorious for stolen cars from Birmingham being dumped and set on fire. As with all things that are constant, complacency can set in. The Fire Service sent a pump to Icknield Street early one morning to a car fire in a gateway. As this was a regular occurrence, they did not inform the Police, but merely extinguished the fire and returned to base. Later the next morning, a dog walker came across the burnt-out wreck, and noticed the charred remains of a dead body in the boot of the car, and alerted the Police. The body was that of a man, and its arm and legs were tied up. It turned out that the body was, in fact, the owner of the car. He was identified as a loan shark, and he had been lured to an address away from our area, murdered by a debtor, placed into the boot of his own car, driven to Icknield Street and the car torched. Members of the Fire Service who attended the scene were disciplined for not finding the body.

I don't know if there were any sackings

on that occasion. (It is standard practice now to check any car fire for bodies.)

I have attended many a road accident and I have seen many gruesome sights. The worst one involved a pedestrian on the A435 dual carriageway. It was winter time, and probably late 1990s. I don't think I had been moved to Wythall at that time, I think I was still at Rubery. I was with a PC Lee (now Chief Superintendent.) It was about half past five in the evening, it was dark and it was rush hour.

On the A453, just a few hundred metres from Becketts Island, is a Texaco garage. The dual carriageway at this location is a national speed limit road and there is no street lighting, so the area is dark. The central reservation is a fairly narrow strip. Lee and I were on patrol in the Alvechurch area when the control room called the Wythall crew to attend a reported road accident at the A435. The Wythall crew were unable to attend, as they were already committed elsewhere. The control room were asking for any available crew to attend. Lee and I shouted up that we would go. We had no information as to what was involved, and neither did the control room.

We entered the A435 from Becketts on the south-bound carriageway, and we could see in the distance a stationary AA van on the north side in the outside lane, with its hazards on. There were cars whizzing past him in the nearside lane. We needed to pass the scene to take the next turning, in order to get onto the north-bound carriageway. As we drove past, we could see one or two cars stopped in the outside lane in front of the AA van, and we first thought it was a minor shunt, because we couldn't see any damage. Having got back onto the north-bound carriageway, we pulled up behind the AA van. It was pitch black, and we put on our blue lights. There was a man in the nearside lane attempting to flag down cars, that continued to whizz by on the nearside, but they were beginning to slow down now that our blue flashing lights were in play.

We asked what had happened, and the AA man pointed to the road surface to the front, and with our torches and headlights we were confronted with a severed leg, and a few yards ahead was a torso with one arm attached, and strewn all up the carriageway was what I would describe as the person's internal organs. We then noticed there were quite a lot of cars all stopped on the nearside of the road, and on the central reservation opposite the Texaco garage, were two shopping bags containing goods from the Texaco store. It soon became obvious we had a fatality, which required the scene to be preserved and meant closing the road. We immediately asked for assistance to close the road, and we managed to stop the traffic.

The pedestrian had been hit by several cars, and then the body run over by several more, some at speeds of 70 MPH or more. There were body parts all over the place, there was a large amount of blood and internal organs spread across the road's surface. We had no idea of the sex of the victim, and there was nothing in the shopping bags to suggest who the person was. There were no other buildings in the area, and despite our best efforts with searching, we could not find a head. The air unit attended the scene and used its night sun, the large beam of light at its front. It lit the area up for us, so we could search the surrounding ditches and hedgerows to try and locate the victim's head. We never found it, and we can only assume it got pulverised by the cars running over the body. A response team attended and took on the role of investigating the accident. The scene was also attended by the Accident Investigation Unit from HQ. Their role was to examine the scene, collect evidence, and prepare plans. A fair number of cars that had stopped had run over the body. Their cars had to be examined and the drivers all had to be interviewed, and the coroner was informed, in order to maintain continuity. All the body parts were pieces of evidence and had to be collected, bagged and labelled and transported to the mortuary at Redditch. For continuity purposes, Lee had the task of going to the Mortuary with the parts and recording the pieces onto the official paperwork.

Lee did not finish until late that night. The body was later identified as an elderly woman from a nearby mobile home site. She had been in Texaco getting some shopping, and she had crossed onto the central reservation. We assumed she either fell into the road, or stepped onto it in front of passing cars. Her son eventually identified her by the ring on her finger. That was the worst accident I had attended. Lee and I, as well as others who attended the scene, were asked to go to a critical debriefing a few days afterwards.

This type of debriefing takes place when someone has been involved in this kind of incident. Not just accidents, it could be anything that might be traumatic, such as having shots fired at you, or indeed, anything really that could cause trauma. Lee and I went, but in those days, after so long in the Service, I was hardened to this type of event, and it did not really affect me. Or at least I don't think it did, and yet here I am, writing about it, as if it is still there in my head.

Of course, Police Officers are not immune to the odd accident. I should know, as my reversing skills left a lot to be desired. When a Police Officer has an accident in a Police car, it normally has to be dealt with by a supervisor. At Wythall we had two Police cars. Again, I cannot remember the dates, but we had just taken delivery of a brand new Vauxhall Astra car. It had the new Battenberg markings, a roof-bar type of blue lights, a siren and it was all nice and shiny. It was winter again and the time about six o'clock in the evening. Robbo was in the office doing some paperwork, and I was at my desk.

A recent new transferee from the Metropolitan Police had started in at Wythall. His name was Mark, but he soon picked up the nick name Reg. Reg had been his nickname in the Met, and we had found this out when someone had called the station where he worked in London to get the low-down on him. We were told he was called Reg after a character on the then popular TV programme, The Bill. He was quite taken aback when we started calling him Reg, and he wanted to know how we knew. At first, we couldn't decide if Reg was one of the lads, because he had a strange aura about him. He was short, but quite stocky. He was very respectful towards me, and always trying to please me by telling me what he had done, and asking if he could he deal with this and that.

I was still making my mind up about him, he seemed the keen sort, but gave me the impression he wanted me to notice him more. He was starting to be the object of some pranks by the others, all banter mind you, no bullying. He asked me one day,

"Sarge, could I use the new car to go to Alvechurch, please? I've some enquiries to make there."

"Well, why can't you use the old car that's in the yard?" I asked him, but it was obvious he wanted to drive the new car.

"Okay, then," I said eventually, "but I don't want you smashing it up. We only got it this week."

"No worries, Sarge," he said, and off he went. He had only been gone about ten minutes when he called me up on the radio. It went something like this:

"BJ01 over."

"Go ahead."

"Er, could you meet me in Lilly Green Lane?" When you hear that type of request, you just know something's wrong. Straightaway Robbo quipped,

"He's smashed the car up, I bet."

"Why do you want me to meet you in Lilley Green Lane?"

"Er, er, I'll tell you when you get here."

I just knew my new car was scratched or had some sort of damage. Dave and I jumped into the old banger and we made our way to Lilley Green Lane. I wasn't expecting to find what I did. Lilley Green Lane is a country lane with a high hedgerow either side. Reg had managed to catapult himself and the car over a hedgerow, and land on its roof in a field on the right-hand side. The car was a total mess, mud all over it, the roof dented, the sides all dented, and hedge debris all round it. And his excuse? You guessed it, he swerved to miss a dog or a badger. Dave went walking up the lane in the direction Reg had come from, and he found a dead badger at the side of the road. Now that was lucky. The jokes were that he carried a dead badger around with him to use in an emergency such as this.

So here I was, faced with Reg, who on the face of things, had got off quite lightly. Okay, he had a cut to his left ear, which was bleeding, but he insisted he was okay. I looked at the damage to the car, and my first words to Reg were,

"It's going to take a bit more than a bottle Tippex to sort this out." I had no choice but to call this in, and to inform the Duty Inspector, who just happened to be my favourite woman Inspector in charge of the response unit, the one I mentioned earlier, where I ended up being developed. This incident was well before the one that had me being developed. I had already decided that I would deal with this, and I waited for her to arrive. Reg was one of my Officers and I would try and keep him out of the shite.

To me it was a straightforward one-vehicle Road Traffic Collision, it did not involve any members of the public, and the hedgerow was not damaged, largely because the Police car had basically flown over the top of it. (I recall a similar accident in 1977/8 time, where two Police cars were speeding to a job and flew through a hedge, killing some sheep.) Reg needed to go to the local hospital to get his ear sorted out, so I told Dave to take him to A & E. But then the Inspector arrived. She took one look at the state of the car, saw the partly damaged hedge, saw Reg with his cut ear, and wanted an ambulance to attend the scene. Then she suggested Accident Investigation be called from HQ. Accident Investigation only attended scenes of potentially serious and fatal accidents. This did not warrant their attendance, and it would mean bringing the on-call investigator from his home.

I had to say my piece, didn't I, and I told her I thought she was going a little over the top.

Reg did not want the embarrassment of an ambulance, there was the evidence of the badger, which he had swerved to miss, and this was why he'd clipped the verge. I could recount the incident to her in full, and I was happy to deal with it.

She was having none of it, and she said, "We are not doctors. What do you think would happen if Reg had a relapse in the Police car on the way to hospital? Police cars are not ambulances, and we need to establish the facts." As Reg was one of my Officers, I could have dealt with that as his superviser, I told her so, but to no avail, so in the end I just walked off and let her get on with it. It was a case of her being over-cautious, and after this we never really hit it off. From that point on we both only ever communicated when we had to. She obviously had the last laugh later on, when I went through the development stage. Luckily the car was repairable and we got it back about a month later, and, needless to say, Reg was banned from driving it.

I did have to deal with a Police accident involving a response crew, as a result of a Police pursuit that started on The A435 at Beoley, and ended up on the Alcester road at Maypole, before disappearing onto the Druids Housing Estate. It was summer-time and it had happened on my day off, but again, I don't recall the date. It was an investigation that started with not knowing who the offender was, and ended up at Worcester Crown Court. A well-known ne'er-do-well had been to the Village Inn pub at Beoley, and he was drunk and being abusive. The landlord hadn't seen him before, but said the bloke had turned up at the pub in a large black 4x4 car. The landlord called the Police, and they showed up, but just as the offender had left, carrying a half-pint glass from the pub.

An observation message was put out, and a response crew saw the 4x4 on the A435 heading towards Birmingham. At that time, no one knew who the offender was. The car was chased up the A435, and back down it again from Becketts Island, where it U-turned across the central reservation, near to a Texaco garage, and sped along the Hollywood by-pass onto Maypole Island, the border with West Midlands Police. It went around the island and forced a couple of cars to crash into some metal barriers, about three hundred yards further on. The car went left through a gap in a hedge, drove across a children's play area, and disappeared into the maze of side roads on the Druids Heath estate, a large council area that has a mixture of houses and tower blocks. The pursuing Officers had to abandon the chase, because of the risk to public safety. The two cars that had been forced into the metal railings were identified, and details obtained. West Midlands Police were informed, as this was on their area, and because it all involved West Mercia, it was decided that we would take on the enquiries and investigation.

A package was prepared by the two officers involved, and it was passed to me to deal with, although I would usually have expected the Duty Response Sergeant to manage this. Anyway, an Inspector had decided the Wythall Sergeant would do it, as I found out the next morning, when I arrived to find the package on my desk. There were statements from the Officers, and I believe one or two statements from the persons in the accidents at the Maypole, and a brief of the events. I already had details of the make, model and the registration number of the car, and we soon discovered it had been involved in petrol thefts at the Texaco garage a few days earlier. I tasked someone to go and get me the CCTV from the petrol station. I first needed to find the car, and I had an idea the offender was from the Druids Heath. From enquires at the pub, I knew I was looking for a fairly tall white man in his thirties.

My first call was to the air unit and I asked if they would go up and have a look over Druids Heath to try and locate the vehicle. We knew the Druids, as it was known, was quite a large estate, with a lot of cul-de-sacs, and footpaths, a good place to hide a car. Within the hour, the air unit had arrived overhead and called me up to say they had found the car. I went straight to the location and the air unit was hovering overhead. The car was unlocked, there was damage from where it had hit the other cars, but the most interesting item in the car was an empty beer glass, which I knew had been in the hand of the offender when he left the pub, as the witness statements had told me.

We seized the beer glass and the car to be forensically examined as evidence. The helicopter and Police activity caused the locals to gather round and, of course, they wanted to know what was going on.

We started asking them if they knew whose car it was, and someone came forward with a name. They'd apparently seen this person arrive the day before, park the car and run off into the estate. I recognised the name given to me, because he was a known criminal with connections in the past to a man we all know to be Irish Tony. Irish Tony had a unit in Portway, not far from Beoley, where he used to do up old bangers. He had a reputation for being a hard man, and according to local intelligence, he had a friend he called Betsy; Betsy was a sawn-off shot gun. Word had it, if you crossed Irish Tony, you would be introduced to Betsy. Now, the name we'd been given of the driver of this car had been a victim of Irish Tony's a couple of years earlier. He had stolen something from him, and Tony repaid him by biting part of his nose off, but he wouldn't make a complaint. No one would make a complaint against Irish Tony for fear of retribution. So now I had a name, but I needed evidence, and the person who gave me the name wouldn't make a statement. The glass was taken away by a Redditch Scenes of Crime Officer called Jim.

I told Jim I wanted him to try and get a DNA profile off the glass, and any fingerprints, plus any evidence from within the car as well. We took statements from the people in the pub, including the landlord. We also looked at CCTV of the two or three petrol thefts, but to be honest, all we could see was a figure with a cap on. I was also contacted by a woman who lived in Wythall, who knew the person we were looking for. She told us he had been bragging about the chase, and that he thought the Police had no idea it was him.

As part of my investigation, I went to Halfpenny Green airport and went up in the Police helicopter to video the route of the pursuit, and when we got over the place where the car had driven through the hedge across the children's play area, we could see from up high, the wheel tracks across the grassed area. A copy of   the video formed part of my evidence. It took a few weeks before the results from the beer glass came back, and it was a hit on the suspect. We now had the evidence to go and arrest him. So early one morning, about five of us paid him a visit. He lived on the Druids, and I think he was half expecting us, because he didn't give us any problems, and he came quietly. We made a search of his address, looking for any keys or documentation relating to the car. He gave a no-comment interview with a solicitor present, and he was released on Police bail, so we could send a file of evidence to the Crown Prosecution for a decision.

Before that, though, I needed a statement from the scenes of crime Officer, Jim, about the seizure of the glass, and his submission of it to the lab. His statement was vital to show continuity. I had a problem in that Jim had fallen foul of the Political Correctness Brigade, this rearing its ugly head at the time. Jim was a cheerful character, always sharing a joke and making innuendoes, but the problem was that he made a comment to the wrong person and they reported him. Jim was made an example of, and his employment was terminated. I went to see him and asked him to help me with the case, as without his statement, the case would fold. Jim was a little bitter, and at first, he was unwilling to assist. I was disappointed, because we'd always got on, and in fact he came to a family milestone birthday of my Mother's, and took some pictures for me. He eventually did agree, though, and he supplied a statement. The case went to Crown Court and as the Officer in the case, I went along, and he was found guilty. The Judge said he was a liar and a thoroughly despicable character, and sentenced him to twelve months' imprisonment.

You always get a satisfied feeling of a job well done when a case goes well.

CHAPTER THIRTEEN
ELECTIONS AND PUSHCHAIRS

Of all the investigations that I have been involved in, two stand out in my mind, and one of these was a first for me, and for my workmates. It was the general election of 1997, when Tony Blair first became Prime Minister.

I was well established at Wythall, and the election itself went without incident. The role of the Police was to maintain a presence at polling stations, and to see that the democratic rights of voters were upheld. The Presiding Officer, i.e. the man or woman nominated as such at each station has powers to instruct a Police Officer to remove persons from the polling station if they are disruptive, or interfere with the election process. Nothing like that happened.

The only incident that came to mind took place at a polling station at Woodrush School in Wythall. Polling finished at ten o'clock that night on the dot, as the Presiding Officer has to make sure it does. One of my Constables, Neville, was on duty at this station, and the doors were firmly shut at ten o'clock, much to the annoyance of a queue of people outside, still waiting to vote. They were vociferous, and one man at the front elected himself spokesperson, complaining to Neville that his democratic right was being denied.

Big Nev, as he was known, was not the sort of person to argue with. Nev was well over six feet tall and broad with it, had a shaven head and could look menacing, but in reality, he was a gentle giant and one of the nicest men I have met. Nev told this man that the station was closed, and he advised him that the choice was his to either go home or go to the cells. The spokesperson, seeing that big Nev was not joking, chose to go home.

The following day, a local resident from an area called Majors Green attended the Police Station, and made a formal complaint that someone had used his vote. He had attended the polling station at Wake Green Football Club, and was denied his vote by the Presiding Officer, as it had already been cast. The offence of personation had been committed by someone purporting to have been him. This was an offence under the Representation of the Peoples Act 1983, a first for me. A statement was taken from him and a crime number generated. The man suspected the offender was the boyfriend of his estranged wife, who he named, and in fact, this boyfriend was from Scotland and not registered to vote in England. His wife still lived in the marital home, and the victim had moved out, but was still registered to vote at Majors Green. I sent the file to CID, as I assumed it was their remit, but it was duly sent back by the Detective Inspector, instructing me to deal with it. I had to do some research as to what was required in order to prove the offence. I discovered that I needed to have sight of the counterfoils from the voting slips. When a person goes to vote, the Presiding Officer tears a ticket from the book and hands it to the person. Each ticket has a unique number, and there is a counterfoil with details that can identify the person voting.

I wanted to know who voted immediately before the suspect and after the suspect, and to do this I needed to have sight of the counterfoils. The problem was that they had all been sent away and stored, as was required by law. The Lord Chancellor's Office at the House of Lords was responsible for the custody of the counterfoils from a general election. I needed to get copies of the offending counterfoil to prove that the ticket had been issued, and it was identifiable to the victim. To get access to the counterfoils, we had to apply to a County Court Judge. The Force Solicitor, Les Martin based at HQ, made the application and the two of us attended Redditch County Court to present our case to the presiding Judge, who granted the order. Armed with the order, I contacted the Lord Chancellor's Office at the House of Lords, expecting the counterfoils to be sent through the post, but I was told I would have to travel to the House of Lords in person, and a representative from the Lord Chancellor's Office would have to be present while I went through the counterfoils.

So a few days later Big Nev and I, donned our best bib and tucker, obtained a railway warrant from admin and off we went to the big smoke. Now, back then I had only been to London once or twice, so I was quite excited to have the opportunity to go into the House of Lords.

I had with me one of those new communication devices called a mobile phone, quite a large object. They were practically as big as bricks in those days. I wanted to be able to be in communication with my office, if not for anything else, to make sure we got picked up at Birmingham International railway station on our return.

So, briefcase in hand, we arrived at the rear part of the House of Lords at the security gate, which was manned by the Metropolitan Police. We were expected, and a nice young man, dressed very flamboyantly, came and met us.

He took us in a lift to an upper floor and then to a small office, where there was a man who knew why we were there. He handed over a box, which contained all the counterfoils from the polling station we were concerned with. I was expecting to be there for some hours, but within ten minutes of looking through the counterfoils, we found the one we were looking for. I wasn't allowed to seize it, but we were allowed to make copies, and then Nev took a short statement from the representative. Once we'd done that, the representative asked us,

"While you're here, and if you've got all you need now, would you like a tour of Westminster Palace? I have time, if you would like to do that."

"Er, yes please." We were delighted to be asked, but it was so unexpected it practically robbed us of speech for a minute or two. He took us on a guided tour of the Palace and gave us explanations about things as we passed them. We were shown the Royal Part where all the carpets and seat covers were coloured royal blue, and the room where Her Majesty is robed before she enters the Lords' Chamber.

We went into the House of Lords, a very grand building with expensive gold leaf all over the place, and he showed us the debating chamber, which was also grand, with chandeliers and other luxurious decorations.

You knew you were in the House of Lords, because the carpets and furnishings were red. There were bars and restaurants in there, as well, for their Lordships.

From there, the representative took us through the main door to the debating chamber into the main hall, where you walk across to the House of Commons, where everywhere is green, and there are no grand decorations. Everywhere is dull and plain, because it is where the Commoners debate. The chamber was in session, and we were taken upstairs to the public gallery to watch the proceedings, which was very informative.

We had to be searched first, even though we were serving Officers, and my briefcase had to be locked away. It was lunchtime by then, so Nev and I thought we'd make a day of it, and take a walk back towards Euston railway station, calling in at some local tourist sights and local inns along the way. It was quite a long walk and made us really thirsty, and we had to keep popping into the buildings called pubs to quench our thirsts.

I remember we had a walk to Westminster, and saw Downing Street, Horse Guards' Parade and Trafalgar Square. We ate in Leicester Square, and saw the actor Martin Clunes walk past the window. It was certainly a different world from the one we lived in. I had lived a very sheltered life up to that time.

We managed to get back to Birmingham International station at about nine that evening, and, using the mobile phone, I summonsed Mark (Tommy)who was on duty at Wythall to come and pick us up.

Armed with copies of the counterfoils, I now had to interview the Presiding Officer and take a statement, exhibiting the counterfoils. Presiding Officers are normally ordinary employees from the local Authority who are nominated for the day. I also identified the persons on the counterfoils immediately before and after the victim's vote. The idea was that they were probably in the queue behind the offender. As it was, the one person whom I interviewed remembered the couple in front of him and gave me a description. Of course, I did have the name of the suspect, but I never did get to meet him or interview him. I now had enough evidence to go and call at the address of the victim's estranged wife. The suspect was not there, as he had returned to Scotland. She provided me with a statement, confirming she had visited the station to vote and the suspect was with her, and he also voted. She maintained she had no idea the suspect had used her husband's vote. Her statement was vital, and I now had enough to interview the suspect under caution. Because he was in Scotland I had to send the file up there, requesting they interview him and report him for the offence, which they did.

I was later told that the suspect appeared before a court and pleaded guilty and, as I recall, was sent to prison for six months. As a uniformed Officer, it's not very often you get plum jobs where you go and travel to see witnesses or go after suspects. CID Officers, however, did often go on their travels in pursuit of their prey.

One of the roles of a Sergeant is to make sure crimes that are destined for further investigations are dished out to the appropriate Officers, those who you know are capable of doing the job. This next investigation of note happened in the early 2000s. I'm not sure now, though, of the exact date. An articulated lorry had been parked up at a transport compound on Hounsfield Lane. It was laden with more than five hundred brand new McLaren Pushchairs.

I allocated this enquiry to Richard (aka Chucky), a very capable Officer. It was obvious the pushchairs had been offloaded onto another lorry, but the problem was the yard had no CCTV, and it was in a rural area. So the chances of finding the culprits or the pushchairs were slim. Until, that is, about a week or so later when a Private Detective entered the Police Station. This Private Detective was an ex-Police Officer from down south somewhere. I had never met a PI before, but I had had ex-Police phone the station before, needing information on people and other issues. I always refused to divulge anything, though, as the Data Protection Act was in place, and it was always rammed home to us about not divulging information. This was not only about personal details, but any details of ongoing enquires, in case it ended up in the wrong hands.

The PI had come to Wythall, as he knew the theft of the pushchairs was being investigated there. Richard was away on leave. The PI explained that he had been hired by security at McLaren. A member of the public had apparently been to a market in North Yorkshire, where a market trader was selling pushchairs. This member of the public was suspicious, and made a call to McLaren about this particular trader. McLaren asked the woman to buy one of the pushchairs from the trader, which she did. Each of the pushchairs had a batch number, and the pushchair she purchased was one of the batch stolen from Wythall. The PI was a very keen man, and he had been hired by McLaren to identify the trader, and to buy another to see if there were any more. The PI had travelled to the same market and got a pushchair which was also a batch from Wythall. He turned up at Wythall and told me all about it, where the suspect trader worked, and he wanted to know what we were going to do about it. He had spoken to North Yorkshire Police, who had batted him back to West Mercia, as we were the Force dealing with the crime.

Dick, my trusted long-time friend, drew the short straw, and sat the PI down and got full details. The PI was keen for action, as the Trader worked the Sunday Market which was next door to Catterick Barracks near the town of Richmond in North Yorkshire. I spoke to CID at Redditch, and the response from them was, "Get on with it." It needed a double West Mercia crew to attend the market at six in the morning on the next Sunday, only a few days away. The Officer on the case Richard (Chucky) was not available, and no one at Divisional HQ was interested, so it was now down to Dick and me to take responsibility. I had never travelled that far north before (that sheltered life again). I was not intending to travel all that way there and back again in a day, especially to make the market for six o'clock. I had to speak to my Inspector and brief him, and he told me to go up the day before, book a hotel and get admin to authorise a hire car. I contacted Richmond Police Station and spoke to a Sergeant who ran a small unit of Officers. The unit comprised about four Constables plus the Sergeant. They were like a proactive trouble-shooting unit.

I fully briefed them and arrangements were made for me and Dick to meet the unit at our Travelodge hotel outside Richmond at a place called Scotch Corner. We arrived in the afternoon and met up with the North Yorks Officers. They were fully briefed and an action plan was put in place for the next morning. We had a list of the batch numbers for the pushchairs, and explained whereabouts on the pushchairs the numbers could be found. They then took us into the town of Richmond and we had a meal and a few bevvies, before retiring to our hotel for a night's sleep, as the next day was expected to be a long one, what with having to travel back to Wythall as well.

Up early, we drove to Richmond Police station, linked up with the North Yorks unit and got to the market at about half past six, just as the traders were setting up their stalls. We identified the trader, and took him to one side. He had a number of McLaren pushchairs identified as stolen, and was arrested by the North Yorks Officers and taken away. There were about twenty of the pushchairs altogether, a small number compared to the more than five hundred stolen. The remaining pushchairs were loaded into a van and we went back to Richmond, where the prisoner had been booked in. Before we interviewed him, we had a cooked breakfast. Dick and a local Officer had a preliminary interview with the prisoner, who was a local, middle-aged man. He seemed quite taken aback when he was arrested, claiming he had no idea the items were stolen. The quick interview revealed that he had bought the pushchairs from a man in a lay-by somewhere south of Yorkshire. They were sold from the back of a large van., and he said that he sold pushchairs at a market behind East Midlands Airport and to top it all, he would be there on that day, as it was a Sunday market.

Now this was not part of the plan. I was faced with a situation where we needed a resource to go to this Sunday market, at the back of the East Midlands airport, and it was about a two-hour drive away, or possibly more. We put an action plan in place. The North Yorks Officers would deal with the prisoner for the offence of handling stolen goods, because we were satisfied he had not been involved in the theft at Wythall. In the meantime, I contacted Leicestershire Police and briefed them and asked for their help. I told them that Dick and I were going to make our way to the market with some local Officers, to whom we'd already given the make and batch numbers of the pushchairs. The local Officers went to the market and identified the stall holder for us.

Dick and I drove down to the site, arriving in the afternoon, when we met with a couple of local Officers. The suspect, a white man in his late thirties, was at the stall, and it had been closed down. The local Officers had identified about twenty or so of the stolen pushchairs, and had seized them. The rest of the pushchairs were looked at, and there were quite a few. By the time we got there, the prisoner was cuffed. We sorted out the pushchairs and transported the suspect to Loughborough Police station, by which time it was five or six o'clock.

Dick and I had been at it now for twelve hours. The Custody Sergeant insisted the prisoner be interviewed that evening, but the prisoner wanted a solicitor, which was his right. We were not going to get home that night. We went and ate, and I contacted the Duty Inspector at Redditch, and fully briefed him, and he authorised for me to book a hotel room for me and Dick. I left Dick to deal with the prisoner while I went looking for a hotel. I found one, the Ramada, and I booked two single rooms. I arranged with the manager that West Mercia Police would pay, but I could not sort that out until the next morning when the finance staff were in.

Meanwhile, back at the station Dick had a preliminary interview with the prisoner, who chose to give a no-comment interview. We established his home address was in Stourbridge, about a seventeen-mile drive from Wythall. The Inspector at Loughborough authorised a section 18 search of his address. This is a section under the Police and Criminal Evidence Act 1984 that allows a prisoner's address to be searched. The address was in the West Midlands Police area, but I wanted my own Officers to attend.

I rang Wythall and I spoke to Richard (Chucky), who had returned from leave, and was working a two till ten shift. He drove with another Officer to the prisoner's address. His wife was in, and they could see a couple of new pushchairs in the porch. These turned out to be from the Wythall batch, and they found a load more in his garage, all stolen from Wythall. They seized the lot and took them back to Wythall. We questioned his wife, and she revealed that the prisoner had a brother with a baby supply shop in the Walsall area, and she even supplied the address to Rich.

We interviewed the prisoner again about the discovery of the stolen pushchairs, and he was asked to account for them being at his home address. Again, he gave a no-comment interview. The time was now close to midnight and I told the Custody Sergeant we needed to rest. I also intended to have the brother's shop in Walsall searched, but I needed a warrant, and that had to be applied for in Walsall. I was aware that the prisoner's wife might alert his brother, but I still had to go through the motions. In hindsight, I wish I'd forewarned the night shift at Walsall to keep a passing watch on the shop to see if there was any activity of removing stock. The prisoner was put to bed for the night, and Dick and I went to the Hotel, where a couple of large whisky drinks with our names on were waiting for us.

My head was buzzing all night, because I needed to get a warrant urgently and get the shop in Walsall searched first thing in the morning. At six the following morning I was on the phone to Walsall Police Station, where I spoke to the Duty Inspector, and spent about half an hour telling him all about the previous day. In short, he agreed to get a warrant organised, but of course, we would have to wait until after nine o'clock for a magistrate. It was all very frustrating and time was passing by, and my hopes of recovering further stolen pushchairs were dwindling. I was convinced there would be some found there. Dick and I were back at Loughborough for nine o'clock. The prisoner had a further interview about his brother's shop, but again, a no-comment interview.

West Midlands Police did not manage to get the warrant until late morning and they searched the shop, but although there were pushchairs for sale, none were the stolen ones. I'm convinced that some would have been found, but for someone tipping the brother off and giving him the chance to get rid of them before the police visit. Naturally, however, I couldn't prove it. The prisoner was released on Police bail to attend Redditch Police Station within a month or so, so that the Crown Prosecution Service could decide if there was enough evidence to charge him.

As it turned out, they decided there wasn't enough evidence to bring charges for the offence of handling stolen goods, or the original theft, so he more or less got away scot free. As for the prisoner in North Yorks, he had no previous convictions and he was unknown to the Police. He admitted the offence of handling stolen goods and was given a formal caution. To top it all, we in West Mercia got no detections and the original theft from Houndsfield Lane was filed undetected. A lot of work and stress for nothing, although we did recover about 80 pushchairs, and Dick and I got recognition for this by way of a Divisional commendation.

CHAPTER FOURTEEN
CAMARADERIE

One thing I loved about the service was the camaraderie. The humour, the banter the closeness of those you worked with, the team spirit and the sense of responsibility towards your fellow officers.

Throughout this book, I have talked about some of the pranks, and a good many of them took place during my time at Wythall. The beginning of the last chapter told the funny tale of Lincoln being drenched. That did make us laugh. Whichever Police Station I worked at, there was always a sense of camaraderie; yes, there were some people who clashed, and this was expected, because, we are all human after all, and clashes do happen, no matter what profession people are in. Wythall was no exception, and I spent nine years there as a Sergeant before I retired, and I had Constables come and go.

One I especially remember was Mark, although universally known as 'Tommy". Tommy was there when I first arrived as the Sergeant back in 1996. He had a reputation for being a prankster, and was always one for drinking lots of tea. His main role was that of Community Officer, and he mainly worked with groups and attended meetings. Tommy and I often went out on patrol during the day, targeting hotspots where crime was known or likely to happen. Mark often found it amusing to see other Officers in awkward positions. An example being, one day we were out in the rural area around the outskirts of Wythall. There had been some house break-ins, and we would often drive around or park up in a prominent area, letting any passing criminals know that we were about.

I'm sure anyone reading this will have heard of the rock group Black Sabbath. Tony Iommi, a member of the group, lived on our patch. I met him once, he was a very nice man, and very approachable too. We often parked outside his main gate, which we did on this one particular day. The gardener was there trimming the hedgerow, and I recognised him as the retired Principal of a Birmingham Children's remand house called Forhill House, which was in fact, located in the Wythall patch. The gardener was a tall man, and I remembered that when he spoke, drops of spittle would emerge from his mouth, a sort of speech impediment. We had parked up and he recognised me and came over to my door. I was in the passenger seat and Mark was the driver. We were sitting there with the engine off. I mentioned to Mark that he was coming over to speak to us, and explained to Mark about his spittle ways, and suggested we speak a minute or two, and then drive off.

Now, picture the scene, this tall man is bent down with his head just poking into my window, which I'd wound down, and Mark sitting in his seat, looking to the right out of his window, having no input in the conversation I was having. The man began to talk to me about nothing in general. In fact if my memory serves me right, it might have been about the good old days at Forhill House.

Well, I let him rattle on for about two minutes, when I interrupted him and said "I think we've just been called on the radio. Is that right, Mark"? Mark looked at me and said,

"No Sarge, you're okay," then turned away, sniggering to himself, and I continued to get more spittle. I gave it another couple of minutes and I again attempted to get away, saying we had to go, as we had an appointment to see someone, to which Mark said,

"It's okay, Sarge, I cancelled it, we've got plenty of time." That Tommy was a lad.

Tommy introduced me to spoofing. Spoofing is a way of selecting someone to make the tea for the rest of the personnel in the office. It works like this: all those who want a cup of tea had to spoof to see who would make it. Each one of us would have to toss a coin across the room and the coin that landed nearest to the wall would be eliminated, and the last person standing would have to go and make the tea. Spoofing took place a few times during the day.

Wythall once had its very own fart machine. I will admit now, that the fart machine was something I bought back in the day. It was battery operated and had a remote control. It very often found itself taped to the underside of a chair, and some poor person sitting down on it would unexpectedly be blamed for farting. Mark (Tommy) took great pleasure in secreting it under a chair and directing visiting Officers from other stations to that chair. He had the remote in his hand, and once he'd engaged them in conversation, he operated the fart machine. Another of my officers from then are my two good friends, Richard and Dave (Robbo), who I am still in contact with today. 'Mad' Robbo talked in a high-pitched voice when frustrated, and he ranted on about things if they frustrated him, and he always gave stupid answers to reasonable questions. For instance, if you asked him the name of someone, he always gave the reply Harry Belafonte.

One summer, Dave had been on leave for a couple of weeks and was due back in on a two till ten shift. He was responsible for the Alvechurch area, so he would have been coming back to a tray full of paperwork, and be expected to catch up on events in the area for which he was responsible. I was on duty, and so was Tommy. Two other crews, the eight till four, and the late crew, were also in the station at that time. We decided we would all have a wager to see how long it would take Dave to start moaning about the amount of work that had piled up while he had been away, and about what had been going on. Someone decided we would call the wager "How long will it take for

Mad Robbo to go mad?" Using the whiteboard in the office, we used a felt tip pen and drew a madometer, similar to the clapometer from that talent show back in the sixties and seventies. I was the referee, all the others put 10p or 50p into a pot and we decided to run for thirty minutes. Every five minutes I would have to place a mark on a scale of one to ten on the madometer where I thought Dave's level of madness lay at that time. The ones making the bet had to guess where on the scale his level of madness would be after the thirty minutes.

It was all set up ready for when Dave came into the Office. He had no idea what we had done, he never noticed the drawing of the madometer on the white board or the fact that every five minutes I was making a mark on it. We all acted normally, asking if he'd a nice holiday, as you do, while he fumbled through his workload. As the thirty minutes progressed, his voice tone got a little higher and his whingeing started, and after about fifteen minutes, with me getting up and marking the white board, we all started to laugh, and Dave wanted to know what was so funny. Dave saw the humour, and still mentions the "madometer" to this day, and it often comes up when we meet up and talk about those days.

Dick had, and to this day, still has, a reputation for being tight with his money, and never missed a trick when it came to saving money. He was a very resourceful man, and he still is to this day. He will not spend money unless he has to. He used a Hitachi type of case to take his paperwork out with him. One day the handle snapped on it., Now anyone else would throw it away and buy a new one. Not Dick, he made a new handle out of copper pipe, soldered it all and fixed plates and screws. I have to say, he did a good job. I once had a cheap metal aluminium sieve for draining vegetables at home, and the handle which was only spot-soldered on, broke. Dick took it home and riveted the handle back on, and I still have it all these years later. He has a large shed in his back garden and has his own lathe. He makes a lot of things from old bits of wood, and he will always tell people not to spend money on things which he might be able to make for a fraction of the price.

One day in the office someone superglued a 50p piece to the floor next to his desk, ready for when Dick came on duty. It was another set-up and a wager was put on to see how long it would take for Dick to spot the coin and try to pick it up The chairs in the office were the wheeled type. Dick arrived for duty and sat in his chair at his desk, and we all eagerly waited to see how long it would take for him to spot the 50p. We expected he would just bend down to pick it up. In due course, he obviously saw it, but instead of bending down, he slowly shuffled his chair towards it bit by bit, hoping we wouldn't notice. Once he was close enough, he placed his foot over the 50p for a few seconds, had a quick glance around the room, then went for it, only to discover it was firmly stuck to the floor. We all had a good laugh.

One day Tommy and another Officer were beginning to annoy me with a football. They kept lobbing it in my direction over a partition I had in place. I pleaded with them to stop, because I was busy, and told them to get on with their work, but the repetition of the ball hitting my head was somehow amusing to them. So I had to take drastic measures. I plucked my pen knife out of my desk drawer, and when it next came over, I stabbed it, squeezed all the air out of it and threw it back. That seemed to do the trick.

For a short time, Paul (Knocker) of the Newquay trip fame, was posted to Wythall as a Constable, having ended his days on the fast response car. Before joining the Police, Knocker was a milkman, so any messages taken for him when he was off duty, instead of being left on his desk, would be rolled up and placed in a milk bottle and placed beside his desk. He once played a trick on our Special Constable, Sally (she and Mad Robbo ended up becoming man and wife). She was due to come on duty and she was seen to pull into the car park. Now, as the Sergeant, I had possession of the spare locker keys, and we thought it would be a good gag for Knocker to hide inside her locker, which he did. Sally, of course, nearly crapped herself on opening the locker and finding Knocker crouched up inside. From that moment on he was known as Knocker from the Locker.

No one was immune to being the subject of ridicule, and it was all part of the camaraderie and what made a happy environment. It fostered a good team spirit, and it certainly didn't affect the way we worked; if anything, it probably meant that some of the work was done more effectively, just because it was a close team. Sadly, this type of banter and antics is unlikely to be part of Policing life in the same way.

Having a good camaraderie was good, but little things can happen that bring it all crashing down. Something happened one afternoon that involved two Officers. Now, of those two Officers, one took it in his stride, and the other took it badly, and it affected his health so much that he had to take a few weeks off sick with a sort of depression. It all stemmed from an incident they attended as a pair in Alvechurch. I can't recall the actual event, but it involved an older man, and he was not a fan of the Police. He lived in a sort of ramshackle place, with a large yard of some description. Whatever the incident was, the boys had attended it, they dealt with the matter and came away.

Later that day, the man reported the loss of some money, and without any foundation whatsoever, called the Police and said one of the Officers had stolen it, and I seem to recall it was a large sum of money. Now I fully understood that the Police must be transparent and be open and all of that. The two Officers were made aware of the complaint, and they at first shrugged it off as being malicious. Their lockers were to be searched, that was the instruction from the top floor, and the search would be carried out by the Duty Inspector. One of the Officers was now off duty, so the Duty Inspector came to search the locker of the one. The inspector was well known to me, his style was friendly and, he would always back his troops.

He took the Officer into the locker room and asked him to open his locker, which he did, The inspector merely looked around without disturbing much of its contents and told the Officer to lock it again, saying he was satisfied there was nothing untoward in there. When the other Officer arrived for work, another Inspector had come on duty, and this one had a different style. This second Officer was aware that his colleague had undergone a search, and the style of the search, and he was expecting the same treatment. This was not to be, the entire contents of his locker were removed, things like his kit bags, boots, and shoes, and each item was thoroughly searched. Of course, nothing was found and nothing was ever going to be found.

The fact that his locker had been searched differently from that of his colleague had a great effect on him, so much so that I didn't see him back at work for weeks. He had it in his mind that they thought he was a thief. The complaint was investigated and found to be unsubstantiated.

I am pleased to say that this Officer eventually returned to work and managed to put it all behind him, but I should imagine this would be an event that sticks in his mind. He retired some years ago.

CHAPTER FIFTEEN
MORALE
(now banned in the Police!)

During my time as the Sergeant in charge at Wythall, I lived by my own philosophy, which was to always have a happy team, to keep morale high, and to encourage everyone to work together. In general terms that was the case, with one or two exceptions. As part of this strategy we would arrange social events, trips to the dog racing track, going "up town" for drinks and a meal, and one regular event would be all going into Birmingham, having a few beers and ending up at a Balti restaurant in the Digbeth area. The place where we liked to go was called Mokhams. Afterwards we would all pile into the pub next door, I think it was called The George, or the Grapes, where we would join in and have a sing-song with the locals, who were mostly from the Irish Community.

One evening we were all sitting in Mokhams, there was about 14 of us, because we very often had other Police personnel, who knew of our team-building nights, who would tag along. No one ever drove, it was all public transport, mainly the train. On this particular evening there was Dave, who had first worked for me as a Special, and his wife, Tommy, Maureen who started as a front counter clerk at Rubery, Nigel, or "Sticky" of the pedal cycle fame on the miners' strike, and others whose names escape me. There were a number of ladies, some Police and some civvies. We had spent a few hours roaming various establishments, before making our way to Mokhams.

Mokhams was not licensed, so we first went into the pub next door, bought our alcoholic beverages and carried them into the restaurant. We had one long table, and both sides were full, there were other patrons sitting at other tables, and the evening was one of banter and laughter, a little raunchy. Tommy sat next to Nigel, and Tommy had his pint of lager on the table in front of him. Nigel was well known for his sense of humour, and very "individual" personality. Tommy and Nigel were quite close, they went back a long time and had a long history of playing pranks on each other which would often go further than other people were comfortable with. Tommy stood up at the table ready to go to the little boys' room, but before he walked away he gave a general instruction to those around him.

"Make sure he doesn't dip his dick in my beer," he said comically, meaning Nigel.

As Tommy walked away, Nigel asked

"What did he say?" I replied,

"He said you're not to put your dick in his beer." That kind of comment was a red rag to Nigel's inner bull, and he took the quip as a direct challenge. Anyone who met Nigel will know exactly what he did next, so I won't go into the graphic details…

Having done his dirty deed, Tommy returned to the table and sat down and, with everyone watching him and giggling, he picked up his pint and lifted it towards his mouth.

"STOP," I yelled, along with just about everyone else at the table as we fell about laughing.

"Why?" enquired Tommy innocently, pint glass frozen an inch from his lips. Looking around at the others it became apparent that they were happy to leave me to be the bearer of bad news. I politely informed him that his beverage had indeed been stirred by the appendage he had specifically mentioned. With an unconcerned shrug Tommy took a swig, clearly enjoying the refreshing nature of his cold lager despite the hysterics surrounding him. He turned to Nigel and thanked him for improving the taste. Other people in the restaurant also found it quite amusing and the waiters looked a little bewildered. Needless to say, I don't think they knew we were the fuzz. I used to avoid going to the loo with Tommy, because when he washed his hands, he had a habit of cupping them to fill them with water, then depositing the water onto the groin area of your trousers, making it look as if you had suffered an accident.

Of all our team-building exercises, one stands out in my mind the most. In August 2004, a few of us decided on a sea fishing trip to North Wales. A weekend event, which involved four of us: me, Pugsy, Knuckles, and Tommy. Point of reference: None of the others ever answered to their real names. If I were to call them Adam, Al and Mark I would receive strange looks and probably cause some concern that I'd been hit in the head. Pugsy had a relative who had a caravan on a campsite in Colwyn Bay. It was a two-bed van which was our accommodation for the weekend. A day's sea fishing trip had been booked for the four of us, and this was something that neither I, nor Pugsy, nor Al had ever done before; Tommy claimed he was a veteran There was a worry between us novices about sea sickness. Al reckoned he had never been on a boat at sea before, a point he made often and loudly.

"Don't worry!" Tommy told us confidently, "all you have to do is keep your eyes on the horizon and you'll be fine."

The day came and Tommy was the driver. We drove to Colwyn Bay and found the caravan site, and it was massive. All the vans looked the same, so naturally Pugsy couldn't find the right one, and had to phone home to get its location. We found it eventually, and the sleeping arrangements were discussed. Now, normally I am very fussy, and I insisted that as I was the only man of rank present, it was only right that I claimed the single bed. Tommy and Al ended up sharing a double bed. That night we had a few beers and we all retired to our respective rooms. Pugsy shared a room with me and we laughed for the next hour: Through the thin walls we could hear Tommy and Al bantering away as they lay next to each other. All sorts of bickering comments flew between them about their male appendices, and laying ground rules about not touching each other in the night, and not to spoon each other. Next morning, I was up and made tea, and took a cup into Tommy and Al. I also had my camera and took a cracking picture of the two of them lying there. I saw some sights that weekend, besides the two of them lying in the same bed, there was also Al sitting on the toilet with the door wide open, and his trousers around his ankles. He was called knuckles because he is short, stocky, and hairy, with long arms. Now, Knuckles was known amongst the criminal fraternity as a man not to cross, but in truth he is a kind and thoughtful man. Don't tell him I said that.

I remember once finding a report on my desk, typed and addressed to me. It was from Al, and it came around the time that management were telling us all how members of staff were to be treated with respect and dignity. It suggested people should be addressed by their correct names and not nicknames, as it was elitist and unprofessional. I thought their suggestion was impersonal and unreasonable, but hey ho. Anyway, I picked up the report and read the page of text, and I became quite concerned. In the report Al said he wanted it known that while on the surface he was a jovial type of character, he was aware that his stature and looks made him stand out from the crowd, and that he was perceived to look like a member of the ape family. The name Knuckles had become an insult to him, which he found very hurtful and offensive. As I read through the report, I thought about how I was going to tackle this, as Al was one of the main culprits for handing out the good-natured insults to others. Was he hiding behind the facade? Was something inside eating away at him? Was he looking to me to stop everyone calling him Knuckles? I grew ever more concerned until I got to the last line.

He had signed it "yours, Knuckles".

The sea-fishing trip day arrived. We didn't have any fishing gear as we were assured it would all be on the boat. We did, as I recall, take a sandwich, and we were dressed in casual clothes like jeans, trainers and a top, maybe a light coat. We arrived at the quay, waiting for the boat to come in. There was a group of four other men, from Liverpool, who we discovered would also be on our boat. They were obviously experienced at this sort of thing, because they were wearing water- proof leggings, waterproof tops, wellies, rubber gloves and towels. This is where it started to dawn on me that maybe we weren't all that well prepared. We'd be fine, we reassured each other.

Along came the boat and it was not what I had expected. It was a small vessel, with a cabin just big enough for the skipper, and the rest of it was open-backed, with bench-type seating across the middle and round the edge. It could hold about eight people, and that's how many of us there was. The sea was quite calm, I did have a few worries, as I didn't want to be sea sick, but Tommy was there on fine form, dishing out his wisdom and past experiences.

"Did I mention I've never been on a boat before?" said Knuckles nervously from behind us.

Off we set and we sailed away from the quay for a good half hour or so. The boat had an engine, so moved fairly quickly, and I could see the land getting further and further away. This was a trip that was to last a good six hours. The skipper was a man in his forties, he owned the boat and this was part of his living, so he had good sealegs, and he didn't talk much. He took us out to a spot where he said we would catch fish, and he gave us rods and a bucket of bait. The idea was that if you caught any small fish, you cut them up and put them onto the large hooks at the end of the line and cast it back in. Well, we started and, yes, we caught a few small fish, mainly mackerel. Of course we hadn't come prepared, no rubber gloves, or waterproofs, no towels to wipe our hands. There were fish juices and water now sloshing about on the boat, and within the hour I was getting bored and cold.

The winds started to pick up and the boat began gently bobbing from left to right, the guys from Liverpool were pulling in some big fish, and we were just managing to get small stuff. I began to feel a little queasy by the second hour, so I decided to just sit on the edge, holding my rod over the side, and not even bothering to reel it in. I was just praying for the time when we could head back to shore.

Pugsy started to look very pale and was

sitting quietly, like death warmed up. Within the third hour he was leaning over the side of the boat, throwing up violently, the contents of his stomach hitting the sea and attracting the small fish to the banquet he was providing. Tommy, for all his brave words of wisdom, was sitting at the side. He was as white as a sheet, and unusually quiet. I have a great picture of him staring blankly out to sea, his skin all swarthy beads of sweat. I thought to myself, "He doesn't look well." Shortly after that, he hung his head over the side and threw up too. I was now fighting back, breathing heavily, praying to the Lord for us to get back to shore. As for the Skipper, he had no sympathy, and when it was suggested we all head back, the firm reply from him was not the answer I wanted to hear. He must have seen this type of thing many times.

After about five hours of hell, the winds picked up even more, the sky was darkening and the boat began to sway a lot more. The waves were getting bigger, the Skipper emerged from his cab and looked around, commenting that the weather was changing and he was heading back to the quay. "Thank God for that,"

I thought. Pugsy had thrown up some more, Tommy managed to hold on, but he was still as white as a ghost. Knuckles, in stark contrast, was having a whale of a time. He thought it was great, and was happy to carry on with a fishing rod in one hand and a soggy sandwich in the other, as he stood swaying on the roiling deck of the small boat, wearing an impossibly large grin.

"I've never been on a boat before!" he reminded us pointlessly.

Arriving at the shore, I vowed I would never do anything like that again; I was cold, miserable and feeling queasy. To this day, I have no idea how I managed not to throw up. Having got ashore, I thought we would all make our way back to the van and recover, but Tommy, within a couple of minutes of landing, decided he was now fine and went and got a burger or something.

Morale played an important part in keeping spirits high, and low morale only produced negativity. The few jolly capers I write about are just a few among many, I could recall other pranks and anecdotes. When I joined, most police stations had social clubs that were run by a committee made up of serving

Officers. Headquarters had one at Hindlip Hall with a large dance floor and was a place for the top floor to entertain other visiting dignitaries. The Police Club formed a big part in keeping up morale, and events like discos were held at various times throughout the year. New Year's Eve was a big event, people often had their leaving do there and there was live music, a place the Officer could take his wife and kids, and let his or her hair down. Kidderminster Club was very active; they used to book outside entertainment, low level celebrities, and novelty acts such as hypnotists, and magicians. This seemed to be the norm, encouraged by the top floor; in fact we often saw members of the top floor at these functions. So it was alright in those times, but things were to change, and in my own opinion, not for the better. Alas, these clubs began to disappear, not just within West Mercia, it seemed to have cascaded across other Forces as well.

It was all part of the changing face of the Police Service, as the Force was going through massive changes. Some of the incoming new senior Officers thought the clubs were out dated, and perhaps the costs were too high. Our team events were a way of keeping a close-knit team, and promoting camaraderie. I was aware that other units at other stations did similar things.

It was all for the general good, and it was not unusual when I worked as a Constable at Redditch, to finish a two till ten late shift, all go up to the club, for a swift one, then up to Balsall Heath in Birmingham for a Balti or curry at midnight. We usually went to a place called the Niralda, a sort of an outpost Police Station if you like, used by other shifts as well as members, and our friends from West Midlands Police.

Since retirement I have attended the odd reunion and retirement dos, and am still in touch with one or two who have just retired, or are about to. I hear stories from them of how morale is at an all-time low; the management of today disapprove of Sergeants fraternising with their troops, and one ex-copper told me his Sergeant had actually been banned from mixing socially with his team by their Divisional commander. It is said that the politically correct brigade takes a very dim view when it comes to the behaviour of Officers when not on duty. A lot do not have social media sites, for fear of being caught using a bit of banter that could be used against them.

Like the old dinosaur that I am, I always tell people the years I served were the best. Morale was high, we worked hard, and we played hard, and we watched each others' backs. When I retired, the downward slope to low morale was well and truly taking hold.

CHAPTER SIXTEEN
DIVERSITY AND THE END

Following the report of Sir William Macpherson in 1999 regarding the Stephen Lawrence report, the Police Service as a whole took on board its findings that the Service, as well as other groups, was institutionally racist.

To me this seemed to be the start of the politically correct brigade becoming ensconced within the Police Service. I know it also happened in other public sector institutions, such as the teaching profession, which my wife works in. Diversity courses were started, and Officers of the day, certainly most of my rank and that of Constable, were very suspicious of these courses, which we were compelled to attend, and believed there was a hidden agenda. They lasted a few days, and of all the courses I had been on, the Diversity course was the most unpopular.

There was a general feeling amongst those of us attending, which was that the purpose was to seek out those with personal views of the world which might not be in keeping with those in vogue with management. We were afraid we would be seen as racist or not politically correct. I had never been on a course where the facilitator did all the talking, and hardly anyone participated for fear of saying the wrong thing, in case it went against them.

The Police Force became paranoid, and the media had gone to town on the story and the phrase used. "Institutionally racist" gave the impression that all Police Officers were racist. Prisoners and their lawyers would jump on the bandwagon and it wasn't unusual for ethnic minority persons arrested, or their lawyers, to throw the term into the hat to use as a complaint.

I remember one Officer at Redditch on the response unit, at the time I was being developed. He was on patrol one dark evening and had cause to stop a car. He spoke to a couple of occupants, and one was a black female, and, as I recall, a member of a community group, or she might have been a councillor. She had questioned the Officer as to why he had pulled them over, and she accused him of being a racist, and of only stopping her because she was black. She made a complaint and the Officer became the subject of an enquiry. He was eventually found to have done nothing wrong, but he had a lot of stress. The management chose to go down the route of investigating him, for fear that they might themselves, be accused of a Police cover-up. The politically correct bandwagon did not just lie with the ethnicity of a person, it also went as far as gender, and sexuality of a person. Conduct and remarks made in the workplace also featured.

Now, throughout my story I have talked about the banter and camaraderie amongst the men and women who work closely with each other. Not just in the Police Force. It happened with any group who are a close-knit team, it could be an army unit, the fire service, whatever. I have spoken to many an officer still serving, as I write this, and the same message comes out. It's not the same today, you can't have a laugh, you have to watch what you say and who you say it to. Now, I am not against diversity, and diversity has a place in the Police Service. It has to, if it is to represent a cross-section of society, and I don't mean just sexuality, or ethnicity. In my eyes diversity includes all sections of society from the uneducated to the well-educated. As I write this, there is talk from the College of Policing, which, by the way, was not about in my day, of making a career in the Police Service a degree profession. I have some disagreement with this, and this is my own personal view. I understand there will be those without a degree, selected to obtain a degree during their service, as a sort of an apprentice. This scheme would have put me off, as I mentioned I was never educationally gifted. The concept of holding the Office of Constable was that a Constable was a citizen. Well, a citizen of a country comes from all walks of life, with different levels of education. Yes, I know that more and more men and women out there are at university than there was in my day. I came from a council estate, I had no qualifications, and a lot of the people I joined with had no university degrees either.

We were truly from a cross section of society, there were young Police cadets, who became cadets straight from school, and transferred into the regulars at nineteen. My fear is, if they get their way and only university graduates are accepted, then a lot of young men and women who do not go to university, whether it be because they are not academically able, or because they are too poor, then our Police Service will not be representative of society. In addition to this, the Government continues to persuade ethnic groups to join the Police, and again, I believe if they continue down this road there will be fewer applicants from ethnic groups than there is already, and if there is a need for the Service, it's more diversity.

There will be too many chiefs and not enough Indians. (No pun intended). The service needs street Officers, those who are not career-minded, the foot soldiers, namely the Constable and Sergeants. These people are the real workforce that deal with the public, who get out there dealing with the fights and the drunks on a Saturday night, those who see life for what it is, and what's more, who have some common sense. And you don't need a degree for this. The graduate Police Officer won't be looking for a thirty five-year career doing this type of work, there will be too many looking for senior level, and when they find they cannot all be up there, they will soon be off to the private sector. When I joined, I saw the role as a privilege and a vocation. The Government, with all its reforms and interference has destroyed this notion, and today it is just a job like any other job.

In short, the Police Service I joined is no longer here.

Don't get me wrong, I enjoyed my thirty years and six months in the Police Service, but the day I left was not the way I wanted to go. I became a victim of the politically correct brigade, and I chose to walk away from the job that I loved. I still speak to and regularly meet up with people I worked with, and we often say we had the best years, but the job went downhill towards the end. Since I walked away, I have had many an ex-colleague tell me they thought the way I had been treated was a disgrace. I am not the only one to have left the service with regrets, and I could name others who, with thirty years' service, are bitter and disappointed at some, but not all, so-called management people. Some of them lacked inter-personal skills, and were only there to further their careers, and they didn't care who they trod on to get what they wanted. Career Officers were coming through the ranks to senior level, and their ambitions to get as high as they could would mean, for some, stamping down on the lower ranks.

I ended my career one working day in November 2005. I had had the option of retiring on a full pension on 23rd June 2005. There was in place at that time something called thirty years plus. It was designed to retain some experience in the Police Service. The way it worked was that I could claim my pension lump sum payment, and at the same time apply to remain as a thirty year plus Officer. My monthly pension payment would be suspended, until I officially retired, and I would continue as a serving Officer in my rank. All I had to do was go through the swearing-in procedure again in front of a magistrate, which I did on the 24th June at the local butcher shop, because my local butcher was a magistrate. My application was processed, and my reasoning was that If I was no good at my job, the application would have been refused. I was to remain as the Sector Sergeant at Wythall, so in effect I retired on the 23rd June and returned on 24th June on the thirty plus scheme. My pension was secured, and the lump sum in the bank.

To all intents and purposes, I was still required to abide by the Police Discipline Code, even though I was effectively now on a yearly contract. The scheme allowed the Force to review my role on an annual basis. So, in reality, I could continue on until my sixtieth birthday, some nine years later. I always said that I would stay on as long as I could, but if I had any hassle I would walk away. Well I did have hassle and I did walk away. My only regret was that it happened six months after 23rd June.

It happened as a result of a female Police Officer who was not at all happy at being posted to Wythall. The woman in question was also gay, nothing wrong with that, and I mention it now, because as this story unfolds, I am perceived to be homophobic. The fact that she was gay was not a problem to me, there were other gay female Officers on the Division, some of whom I had worked with before and got on well with. The problem was that all the staff at Wythall were young men, a mixture of married and single. There were about ten of us altogether, and there was one Officer at the time who was married and had a circle of gay friends he often talked about.

A transferee Officer from another Force

had not long been posted to Wythall, and he was settling in nicely. Being an all-male domain, as you would expect there was a lot of banter and mickey-taking, which was normally confined to the station. We were a close-knit unit and on the whole, everyone got on well. I was the only supervisor, and our Inspector was based at Bromsgrove. He was a long-standing Inspector of many years, he was easy going and you could talk to him about anything in confidence. The Chief Inspector was a recently promoted man, young and ambitious. At that time, the senior team consisted of a Superintendent, someone I had worked with once when he was a Sergeant, and the Chief Superintendent, who I was a Sergeant with in my Kidderminster days.

The Superintendent was not an entirely popular man with some. He had a reputation of wanting things done his way. Every month all the Sergeants on the sectors had to attend a Divisional Performance meeting. At the meetings, the previous month's detection and non-detection figures would be produced. If a particular sector was not performing well, the Sergeant would have to explain why. Action plans would be put in place. Now earlier on, I mentioned that I could be quite vocal, and if I thought something needing saying, then I would say it. Part of the performance culture would look at arrest rates of certain Officers.

I had occasion once during the six months after 23rd June 2005 to have words with a particular senior officer from the command team on a day when he came on a visit to Wythall. A couple of weeks or so before, one of my Officers, who I won't name to save any embarrassment, had been picked up about the lack of arrests he had been having. Arrest numbers are recorded on the West Mercia system. It did not count any arrests made where, for example, prisoners were taken outside West Mercia. Wythall is located about three or four miles from Kings Heath Police Station, a station in West Midlands area. This Officer, in one week, had about six or eight prisoners, which, in some cases, is more than some Officers have in a year, depending on their role.

Through good Police work, he had stop-checked some suspicious persons in Wythall, who were found to be wanted by the Police. They were, no doubt, in the Wythall area up to no good. They were wanted by West Midlands

Police, so in order to save time and expense, he and his colleagues arrested and conveyed the prisoners direct to Kings Heath, and therefore the arrest records would not appear on the West Mercia system. Normally such people were taken to a West Mercia Station, then West Midlands had to travel and collect them. As Kings Heath was much closer than Redditch station, and to save time, they were transported straight to Kings Heath.

Later that same week, while he was on nights, he followed a suspect car used in a crime, and a pursuit was started. He kept up with the offenders along the M42 motorway, and the pursuit ended in another Force area. He made the arrests of about four people, and took the prisoners into the neighboring Force's custody. Again, this would not be shown on the West Mercia system. These arrests were an example of good Police work, and it does not help the morale of the Officer when he is summonsed before a senior ranking Officer and accused of not working hard due to his arrest rate. I was somewhat annoyed, because this senior Officer should have spoken to me if he had a problem with the performance of one of my Officers. I could have enlightened him on the recent arrests he had made as a result of good police work. Instead of that, he chose to simply look at a data draft taken from a West Mercia System.

I had known this senior Officer when he was in the lower ranks. I made it clear to him that I thought he had treated the Officer badly, and pointed out to him the excellent piece of Police work he had done, and the fact that just because the figures didn't show on the West Mercia system, it did not mean he was slacking. I put it to him that he ought to give the Officer an apology. I was not afraid to speak my mind, and I understand the Officer did get an apology, but the fact that I had spoken my mind may have sown the seed in his mind that I had to go. I may be wrong about that, but what followed in the coming weeks convinced me it did.

The young Policewoman who was to come to Wythall was nearing the end of her probationary period; that's the first two years of her service. I had not met her before, but it was my understanding, from what I had been told prior to her arrival, that she had made it known she wanted a career in CID. She had not even completed her two-year probation period, and yet here she was making it known she wanted to get into CID. Getting into CID usually did not happen until you had some experience behind you. My Inspector had given me the nod to say she was being posted to Wythall to get some experience of rural Policing as part of her development, and he advised me that she was ambitious and did not want to come to Wythall. I made sure the men at the station were aware of this, and some of them told me they knew of her, and she had a reputation of being a politically correct sort. There was also mention of her sexuality. I made it plain that the banter and so forth of the male staff had to be toned down in her presence. I decided to team her up with the transferee, who by that time had been with us for a month or two. He was a mature-minded person, and tactful, and I thought it might be good for her too. Normally we found that anyone posted to Wythall for the first time would rather not be sent there, but did in the end get to like the place, and I was hopeful she would too.

On her first day, I had a chat with her,

when she told me she had ambitions to get into CID. I asked her to look upon this posting as a stepping stone towards her goal, and said I hoped that she would soon settle in. I also mentioned to her that she now found herself in a male-dominated station, and she should not take any flak from anyone, and if she had any problems, she should let me know. It was explained to her that Wythall was a one-Sergeant station and as I was not there all the time, she would very often have to make her own decisions.

Every November, usually the first Saturday in the month, Wythall Community Association held the annual bonfire and firework display. This event attracted a large crowd, even visitors from over the border came onto the local park. Rest days at Wythall were normally cancelled for the event, as in previous years there had been a few problems from youths from over the border coming to fight local youths. All went well, the bonfire went ahead as planned, and about thirty minutes before knocking-off time, a job came in somewhere which required two Officers to stay on and deal with. This Policewoman was not on a rest day working, and I asked her and the transferee to stay on a couple of hours to deal with the job. They both refused and I explained that someone had to do it. I did not want to order them to, as I had a right to do, and in fact I had never ordered anyone to do anything in the past.

It became obvious to me that neither he nor she was keen, and I ended up having to stay on myself with one of the others. This was something that had not happened before at Wythall, as normally we worked as a team, we had a sense of ownership for the place, and if a job needed doing then normally someone would take it on. (This is what I mean about the job being a vocation, you just got on and did it.)

This was about three weeks after she had started, she was not settling in, and I could sense she was not happy; I also had the feeling that she did not like me. Perhaps she was not used to my style of supervision, I don't know, I never did put my finger on it. Wythall Station building was not like any other station. Originally it was a small office with two houses either side. The main office had six desks, plus mine. I didn't have my own office, because I wanted to be in the main office with the rest of the team. Off the main office was the old kitchen, which was now the men's locker room.

One day, possibly the Monday of my last week in the job, she was on the early turn, eight in the morning till two in the afternoon. At about 1.45pm the two male officers arrived to start the two o'clock shift. One of the Officers was the one who had the good arrests I mentioned earlier, when I had a run-in with the senior Officer. The two of them had gone into the locker room to get dressed into their uniforms, the door was open and you could hear them having some banter between themselves, no swearing or anything like that. She was sitting at a desk almost opposite me, doing some written work, when one of the Officers was spraying himself with a deodorant. The fumes caused the other male officer to cough, and jokingly I heard him say to his mate,

"What the hell is that you're putting on, you poof?" That one word, poof, caused her to lift her head and look straight at me. There was no smile on her face, and I sensed she did not like what she had heard.

I knew straightaway that that one word

had offended her. I just looked at her and tutted and made the comment,

"Huh, boys, they can be children at times, can't they?" She said nothing and went back to her work, the two men began duty and as far as I was concerned that was it. I suppose in hindsight, she expected me to jump out my seat and castigate the two of them, but that wasn't me, that wasn't my style. That night I lay in bed thinking about that short moment and, reflecting on it, I knew she was looking to me to tackle them for saying that word. I did speak to them that same day after she had gone home, but they couldn't see that they had done anything wrong as it was just a bit of banter.

The next morning, I sat the female Officer down, and asked if she had been offended. I explained to her that it was banter, and I apologised to her and said she must speak up if she had any concerns, and I would address them. She never said much, but the vibes I got from her told me she did not like working at Wythall. About two days later I arrived at work at eight in the morning. The female Officer was due to be on at the same time, but she did not turn up. I thought she might be caught in traffic or something, so I wasn't too concerned. At about quarter past eight, the phone rang, and it was the Senior Officer for Bromsgrove. He told me that the female Officer wouldn't be coming to Wythall that day, as he had a special job he wanted her to do, and he just wanted to let me know.

I began to get the feeling something was not right, and I feared he wasn't being truthful with me. About ten minutes after that, my Inspector arrived in my office, and he asked if there was anyone else in the building. He shut the door and told me that the female Officer had made a complaint against me and the two Officers from the other day. She was upset that they had used the word "poof" and I had done nothing about it. She had confided in another female Officer at Bromsgrove as to what to do. She in turn told the female Inspector, the one I've mentioned before in previous chapters. The female Inspector, so I later learned, took her to a member of the management team, the same one I had challenged earlier about the arrest rates. The Officer apparently told this female Inspector we were, or at least I was, a racist and homophobic, and I ran a homophobic station. Of course, political correctness was at its height and West Mercia had recently been sued by a female ex-Chief Superintendent on the grounds of sexual discrimination. Also around that same time, the local Birmingham media was reporting another highlighted case of a West Midlands Senior Detective doing the same against her Force, so I have no doubt the top floor at HQ was all jittery, as were other senior Officers.

By now the message being received by the member of the command team was that we were all homophobic, we hated gays and I condoned my male Officers' use of homophobic words and behaviour in her presence. Once again, the senior Officer did not think to contact me to find out what this was all about, but chose to believe her and instructed that she be taken to HQ that morning to make a full statement to the professional standards department. Meanwhile, it was clear that the telephone call made to me earlier by the Bromsgrove Senior Officer was a complete fabrication, and that she had not been doing a job for him. The whole way this was being handled was, in my eyes, a disgrace. My Inspector had the bottle to come and tell me what was happening, but he did not agree with the way it was being handled. I asked why they had not come and seen me to discuss this, instead of just taking her word for it.

This was political correctness gone mad, the management were obviously frightened. My Inspector suggested to me that there were plans to remove me from Wythall and place me back onto a response shift at Redditch, working twenty four hour shifts. "Not me," I said. I reminded him that I was a thirty- year plus Officer and I always said if I had any hassle, then I was off. I told him I intended to send in my resignation that morning to the Chief Inspector. I was determined to wrong-foot them. I was required to give a month's notice. I had at least twenty one days' annual leave owing to me, and some time off owing to me on the overtime sheet. It meant that I could to finish that morning. By ten o'clock, my resignation and my intention to retire were submitted, and the fact I was owed all this leave meant I could finish that day. I made no mention of what I had learned from my Inspector.

Within thirty minutes of the email sent to him, the C/I called me and asked why the sudden resignation. I did not let on I knew about what was going on, or the fact that my Inspector had been to see me. I made up some excuse that I had been thinking about it, and then he told me there had been a complaint from the Policewoman. I acted all surprised, and asked what it was about, and he again came out with some garb, claiming he wasn't sure, and that he had been instructed by a member of the command team. He did not have the bottle to come clean. In my eyes he was a career man and didn't want to hurt his chances of furthering his career, which to some extent I can understand. After all, Wythall was part of his domain, and all this would reflect on him. He was not going to back me when his loyalties lay with his masters. As usual, I said my piece and told him I was disgusted at what was happening, and that this woman's allegations were being taken as read.

I told him I was going home and suggested he got another Sergeant to oversee Wythall. With that I went home and I never returned from that day.

I had a phone call from the Chief Inspector the next day to tell me that the Deputy Chief Constable (DCC) had rejected my retirement letter, as there was an active complaint against me being investigated. I reminded the C/I that the DCC could not stop my retirement, as I had retired six months previously, and was reinstated on the thirty-plus scheme. Meanwhile the two Constables that started all of this were also served with disciplinary papers over the use of the word "poof". I was in regular contact with the Officers at the station, and within two days we were all off duty and met at a local pub to debrief on everything that had happened. Most of us were there, making about ten of us in that pub. We were all off duty and we were huddled in a corner.

The two Officers concerned were there and we couldn't understand what the hell had happened. We all agreed she had been manipulated in some way into making the complaint. We didn't think she would have done it on her own, and thought she was being railroaded into it, or at least that was my belief. There was a mole amongst us in that meeting, because what was said in that pub was fed back to professional standards. So I found out the next day. The day after that, I was at home and a Police Federation rep, someone I had worked with at Bromsgrove, telephoned me. I was taken aback when he told me that the DCC had been informed of the meeting in the pub the night before, and that someone at that meeting had reported back, suggesting there was a plot to deny the word "poof" was used, and that it was a case of her word against that of the two Officers.

Talk about being stabbed in the back.

It was not true that a plot was being hatched. It was all bravado, and the two men involved decided to take what was coming from the command team. I do not know who the mole was, but I have my suspicions. There were about eight or ten of us in that pub. In later years, I met up with the Federation rep, who is also now retired, and I asked who the mole was. He claimed he couldn't remember, bless him. I'll give it another few years, and perhaps he will remember then. I was also told that the DCC was in a fix, because he had a serious allegation that I ran a homophobic Police station, and that I was a homophobe. He accepted I had already retired and that they couldn't keep me on, so he agreed to let me go, providing I put in a report explaining my side. Now If I'd wanted to, I could have been bloody minded and told him to stuff it. I was persuaded, however, that this was the best cause of action, and he arranged a local Federation representative to assist in compiling a report. A fellow Sergeant came to my home and together we worded a report.

This woman who stood accusing me of being a bigot and a homophobe knew nothing about me. Had she bothered to ask, I could have told her that earlier I had been present at the civil ceremony of two men I have known for many years. My wife and I had also spent time on holiday abroad with them, celebrating our 25th wedding anniversary. The New Year's Eve before that, we had two gay couples at my home for the New Year celebrations. I am not, nor ever have been, a homophobe, and had the Command Team Officer bothered to pick up the phone and ask me, then perhaps none of this would have happened. The whole matter was blown out of all proportion, on the say so of one female who had been manipulated by others, who I believe did not think highly of me. Officers at Wythall were interviewed by

Professional Standards and were asked directly if I was a racist and homophobic. It was not the way I intended to go, and I am very sad that my career had to end this way, and I was not the only Officer who did end their careers like this. I know of two other Sergeants who were close to retirement, who also left with bad feelings against the same management team. One was a Custody Sergeant, who had done that job for a long time. While he was in custody, a lot of changes in laws and procedures had taken place, and if he were to go back on the streets, he would have struggled. He was, like me, in his fifties. It was my understanding that he, too, would say his piece if he had something to say. The best way to make someone go is to upset them. He was told he was being put back onto the streets after many years in custody. He ended up having to go off sick with stress, again another example of management treating the lower ranks with contempt. I can think of others as well, but that is their story and not mine.

I do not hold any animosity towards the people I worked with. There were good times and there were bad times. The people were a mixture of good and not so good. In the last ten years, I have attended many a reunion or retirement do, and it's been good to catch up with those I have worked with.

At my own retirement party, held late January 2006 (I did not arrange it, it was arranged by my good friends Maureen Townsend and Stu MacDonald) people there made references to the way I had been treated and the circumstances under which I left. It was my 'Wythall Gate' moment, and I know this incident rumbled on, because I have spoken to an Officer who joined a few months afterwards, and he knew about 'Wythall Gate'.

I still see some of them on social media, and as I write this, one of my ex-colleagues is decorating my house. Since the day I walked out, I have been self-employed carrying out investigation work on behalf of the Motor Insurance sector. I take statements and go to the scenes of accidents to prepare sketch plans and take photos. It is a very enjoyable job. As for the Policewoman who started the end of my career, well, she got her role in CID in the end, but I am told she herself was the subject of a complaint. I don't know the ins and outs, but she eventually left West Mercia and transferred to another Force.

Two of the Command team running the Division about a year or so after I left were subject to an enquiry into the way they managed the Division. I was told there were complaints about their style of management.

The Bromsgrove Commander has since been promoted and moved on, and no doubt my incident was put onto his CV as a management incident he had dealt with. My Section Inspector eventually retired well after his time. I have not seen him since, and I believe he moved away to be near his daughter.

The two Constables who were the subjects of a discipline case were interviewed about the incident, and as part of their interviews, they were asked questions about me; was I racist, and was I homophobic? It is a fact that these allegations were made about me without any substance.

Am I bitter? No not at all, but I feel very sad that the Policewoman appeared to have been manipulated. I am now a member of West Mercia NARPO, the National Association of

Retired Police Officers. I attend the two annual NARPO dinner functions each year and I also go the Annual General Meetings.

In a way, the incident did me a favour, because I found out that after retirement, whether it happened happily or not, there is life after the Police Service.

I became less stressed and realised that in the later years of my career that I was on a merry-go-round of targets and figures that had all been created by the government of the day. The young Officers of today's modern Police Force would most probably laugh at my generation. I imagine they see us as dinosaurs, we who didn't have stab vests until near the end of my service, and had to march up down parade squares when training. They would roll their eyes when we talk about the good old days, and use that famous phrase of Uncle Albert's from Only Fools and Horses, "during the war!"

Well I see it another way. I may hark back to the good old days where society held a shred of respect for the Police and the job we did, to times when we didn't need stab vests. I regard the young Officers of today with a hint of sadness, because they missed out on a time when the job was a lifelong career. A vocation. A true calling.

Finally, I would like to thank my wife for her support throughout my career. She had to put up with a lot of long shifts, house moves and at the start of it all, she gave up a job and a house to move to Wellington, and she supported me up to the very end.

My thanks, also to my son Paul for his support, and that of my family, not forgetting to mention my granddaughter Abigail for her input and ideas towards a title for this book. Also the whole team working for and with DHP Publishing; Susan for her expertise in editing, Claire from Spurwing Creative for a great cover and David, who took a chance on me and guided me through the process to get my story out there.

THE END
Thanks for reading!